Alister Ross
1963

ENGLISH SATIRE

THE CLARK LECTURES

1956

ENGLISH SATIRE

BY

JAMES SUTHERLAND

CAMBRIDGE
AT THE UNIVERSITY PRESS
1962

PUBLISHED BY
THE SYNDICS OF THE CAMBRIDGE UNIVERSITY PRESS

Bentley House, 200 Euston Road, London, N.W.1
American Branch: 32 East 57th Street, New York 22, N.Y.
West African Office: P.O. Box 33, Ibadan, Nigeria

©

CAMBRIDGE UNIVERSITY PRESS

1958

First printed 1958
First paperback edition 1962

First printed in Great Britain at the University Press, Cambridge
Reprinted by offset-litho by Latimer, Trend & Co., Ltd., Whitstable

PREFACE

IN preparing these lectures for the press I did not try to remove all signs of their colloquial origin, but I occasionally eliminated an expression that looked too casual for the printed page. While revising the manuscript I also took the opportunity of adding a few afterthoughts. The lectures, however, remain essentially as they were delivered. In the first of them I discussed the nature of satire and the motives of the satirist. It should be obvious that in the other five I did not attempt anything like a history of satire. It is true that I kept to a chronological order in each lecture, and paid some attention to developments; but I spoke only about those satirists who interested me most, or about whom there was something that I wanted to say.

LONDON   J.S.

CONTENTS

I

THE NATURE OF SATIRE

SATIRE has never received much serious attention from English criticism. For one book on satire there are probably half a dozen on comedy, and perhaps as many more again on tragedy. It is true that in recent years there have been signs of an increased interest in satirical writing, but a good deal of the old Romantic prejudice against satire still remains. The satirist is destructive; he destroys what is already there (and what to many people appears to be functioning quite satisfactorily), and he does not necessarily offer to fill the vacuum that he has created. He is, as Mr Kenneth Tynan remarked recently of Bernard Shaw, 'a demolition expert'. We are being grossly irrelevant, Mr Tynan added, 'if we ask a demolition expert, when his work is done: "But what have you created?"...Shaw's genius was for intellectual slum-clearance, not for town-planning'.[1] If the present age is not unsympathetic to intellectual slum-clearance, the feeling that the satirist is somehow negative, uncreative and irresponsible is still there.

There might, however, be more critical discussion of satire if the satirical could be more easily isolated for analysis. When we think of satire we are not usually bringing our minds to bear on some specific form (the satirical poem, the satirical novel), but on some quality which gives a work its special character. Even if we do go on to consider the satirical poem or play or novel, we are not yet dealing with a form which can be easily defined, or which is much more than a convenient category for discussing individual works that may vary widely in structure and tone and even intention. *Hudibras*, *The Rape of the Lock*, *The Vicar of Bray*, *The Dunciad*, *Verses on the Death of Dr Swift*, Samuel Wesley's epigram 'On the setting up Mr Butler's monument in Westminster-Abbey', Johnson's verses on Sir John Lade's coming of age, *The Vanity of Human Wishes*, *The Vision of Judgment*, are all satirical poems, but they have little in common apart from the fact that they are all critical, some more, some less, of actual people or of an existing state of affairs. Some works, again, are satirical throughout; in others the satire is only intermittent, one element in a more complex effect. The lines that separate the satirical from the unsatirical are often hard to define, either because the writer shifts easily and rapidly from one mood to another, or because the satirical tone is so rarefied as to be almost imperceptible. In considering English satire I want to be free to discuss it wherever it occurs. If I were to confine myself to works which are professedly and unmistakably satirical from beginning to end, I should have to ignore some of the subtlest and most penetrating satire in English literature.

The main difficulty, I believe, is to distinguish the satirical from the comic. The writer of comedy is usually dealing with the same sort of materials as the writer of satire. Like the satirist, he is very much alive to the follies and imperfections and faults of men and women; he sees us falling short in one way or another of the standards to which he himself consciously or unconsciously subscribes, or notably ignoring or departing from the conventions which he accepts. He perceives, as Bergson put it,[1] certain rigidities, a certain inelasticity of mind or lack of adaptation in men and women, and in his novel or his play (or, it may be, in his essay on Sir Roger de Coverley or the Man in Black) he exposes them in action. But all this he does, as Wordsworth said of the old farmer of Tilsbury Vale, 'in the ease of his heart'. The writer of comedy accepts the natural and acquired folly and extravagance and impudence which a bountiful world provides for his enjoyment; he is a sort of human bird-watcher, detached and attentive, but no more troubled by moral issues than the ordinary bird-watcher is when the starlings swoop down on his bird table and drive away the tits and the nut-hatch. It is surely in this spirit that Shakespeare watches Falstaff and Sir Toby Belch and Bottom and Autolycus, and it is largely because Shakespeare withholds his moral judgment that those characters are allowed to develop so abundantly, to flower into the perfection of irresponsibility, to belong so completely and unquestionably to folly's idle brood, self-pleasing and quite touchingly self-absorbed. This does not mean that the writer of comedy has no standards or norms; he can only be alive to the eccentric, the abnormal, the imperfect if he is aware of the regular, the normal, and so on. But though he is a balanced and integrated person himself, I have never supposed that he has any vested interest in pushing moral standards; and his attitude to those who fall short of them appears to vary from an amused tolerance to a cheerful or even delighted acceptance. So far as human nature is concerned, he is much more likely to appear as Counsel for the Defence than Counsel for the Prosecution, but his normal position is among the spectators in the public gallery. Although he judges what he sees and hears, he has no

3   1-2

great desire to pass judgment, and still less to strip bare and victimise the intellectual and moral imbeciles he has observed.

It is, on the contrary, the mark of the satirist that he cannot accept and refuses to tolerate. Confronted with the same human shortcomings as the writer of comedy (and with others more serious) he is driven to protest. For him those are not matters for pure contemplation; they must be exposed, held up to derision or made to look as hideous as he believes them to be. 'After all,' Shaw once wrote, 'the salvation of the world depends on the men who will not take evil good-humouredly, and whose laughter destroys the fool instead of encouraging him.'[1] Yet if the satirist is sometimes concerned with sins and crimes almost too serious for comedy, the difference between the satirist and the writer of comedy is not the difference between flagrant sins and trivial faults.

The motives that lead to satire are varied, but there is one motive that may almost be called a constant: the satirist is nearly always a man who is abnormally sensitive to the gap between what might be and what is. Just as some people feel a sort of compulsion, when they see a picture hanging crooked, to walk up to it and straighten it, so the satirist feels driven to draw attention to any departure from what he believes to be the truth, or honesty, or justice. He wishes to restore the balance, to correct the error; and often, it must be admitted, to correct or punish the wrongdoer. We need not take Persius too literally when he says that he must speak out or burst; but much of the world's satire is undoubtedly the result of a spontaneous, or self-induced, overflow of powerful indignation, and acts as a catharsis for such emotions. What, however, distinguishes the satirist from most other creative writers is the extent to which he is dependent on the agreement or approval of his readers. If he is to achieve this catharsis for himself, he must compel his readers to agree with him; he must persuade them to accept his judgment of good and bad, right and wrong; he must somehow inoculate them with his own virus. In actual practice, a minority of his readers probably agree with him already; the great majority are either quite indifferent and must be aroused, or they are actively hostile and must be converted.

The art of the satirist, then, is an art of persuasion, and persuasion is the chief function of rhetoric; indeed, the first definition that the *Oxford English Dictionary* gives of rhetoric is 'the art of using language so as to persuade or influence others'. I take satire, therefore, to be a department of rhetoric. Where the writer of comedy is content to interest and amuse, and to fashion delightful patterns out of human character and action, the writer of satire is trying to persuade men to admire or despise, to examine their habitual assumptions, to face ugly facts, to look beneath the surface of things, to change sides in politics or religion, to return to the old and true, to abandon the old and outworn, to do this or to do the exact opposite—in short, to see, or think, or believe whatever seems good to the writer of satire. It is, then, the satirist's *intention* that differentiates him from most other writers; and though individual satirists vary greatly from one another in temperament, and so may be quite unlike in their method and approach, they have in common the practical intention of working upon the mind of the reader so as to influence his attitudes and beliefs, and ultimately, it may be, his actions. No wonder the satirist is unpopular in many quarters; he comes round knocking us up from a comfortable sleep to face hard and uncomfortable facts. Later, we shall have to distinguish the satirist from other writers who set out to persuade us, such as preachers, the author of *Pilgrim's Progress*, political journalists, and so on; and again we may find the precise dividing line between one kind and another rather hard to draw.

How important the intention is when we are trying to discriminate between comedy and satire may be illustrated by a news item that appeared recently in a London newspaper, the *Daily Express*:

Forty-three year old Mrs M—— H——, fined £5 at Lambeth yesterday for stealing a 6s. 6d. slice of veal from a Brixton self-service store, said: 'The public should be protected from this kind of shop. They put temptation in your way, then the blame is put on you, and not the shop.'

That, I submit, is comic. We admit the moral eccentricity, but we recognise the psychology, and we salute the resurgence of the human spirit in difficulties. I could easily imagine Falstaff protesting in very similar terms to the Lord Chief Justice if he had been caught lifting a sirloin from a butcher's stall. Yet when this news item was reprinted where in fact I found it, in the well-known column called 'This England' in the *New Statesman*, the effect was somewhat different. The account of the Brixton woman had now become satire, or something like it. It had become satire because we were being invited to read the passage as yet another exposure of the English character; our laughter was being solicited, and we were expected to laugh with the critical condescension of a good *New Statesman* reader. In any case we had come already prepared to scoff, for as

6

habitual readers of 'This England' we turn to each week's instalment with our minds primed for the sort of thing we are to expect.

If we can agree that it is the satirist's intention—to expose, or deride, or condemn—that distinguishes him from the writer of comedy, then we shall probably find that much of what has conventionally been referred to as comedy should more properly be called satire. If we seek help from the literary critics, we shall find many of them making claims for comedy which seem to be more appropriate to satire. Not to go further back than the Italian critics of the Renaissance, Trissino assures us that tragedy and comedy both aim at teaching, and that comedy teaches 'by deriding and censuring things ugly and vile'.[1] To our own Sir Thomas Elyot the purpose of comedies is to lay bare evil, 'to the intent that men beholdynge the promptnes of youth unto vice, the snares of harlotts and bauds laide for yonge myndes, the disceipte of servantes, the chaunces of fortune contrary to mennes expectation, they beinge therof warned may prepare them selfe to resist or prevente occasion'.[2] Human nature is infinitely various, and there may have been young men in the reign of Henry VIII who rose from their reading of Plautus and Terence with their eyes opened to the snares of harlots and bawds, and who walked more warily in consequence. I cannot believe that they were numerous, or that they learnt much. Fifty years later, Sir Philip Sidney, who must have known Elyot's *Governour*, and who had certainly read the Italian critics with close attention, came to the defence of comedy in very similar terms. The comic poet, he tells us, deals with 'the common errors of our life, which he representeth in the most ridicu-

lous and scornefull sort that may be, so as it is impossible
that any beholder can be content to be such a one'.[1] Sidney
did not live long enough to see that antinomian old scamp
Falstaff pursuing his career of triumphant roguery on the
London stage; but if he had, it is hardly to be believed that
he would have found the only enjoyable moment to be the
one in which Prince Hal denies his old companion with the
icy words:

> I know thee not, old man: Fall to thy prayers:
> How ill white hairs become a fool and jester.

Indeed, the very indignation which this speech has aroused
in generations of readers and playgoers is some measure of
the extent to which the common reader does *not* share
Sidney's view of comedy. The rejection of Falstaff comes as
a shock because we feel it as a rebuke to ourselves. For ten
acts we have been delighting in the adventures of the old
libertine; and if we have not actually identified ourselves
with him, and might not on reflection be altogether 'content
to be such a one', we are certainly content enough that
Falstaff himself should. But if Shakespeare's plays would
rarely have furnished Sidney with the sort of satisfaction he
expected from comedy, the plays of Ben Jonson undoubtedly
would. In Jonson's plays the satirical purpose is never
forgotten.

For a final example of the critic who assumes that the
business of comedy is to satirise vice and folly, we may turn
to the Rev. Jeremy Collier, whose *Short View of the Immoral-
ity and Profaneness of the English Stage* was published in
1698. Collier, a classical scholar, lost no time in making
clear the grounds on which he was going to attack the
contemporary drama. 'The business of plays', he insisted

firmly, 'is to recommend virtue and discountenance vice. 'Tis to expose the singularities of pride and fancy, to make folly and falsehood contemptible, and to bring everything that is ill under infamy and neglect.'[1] Proceeding upon that assumption, Collier has only to quote to prove his case, and he goes on to compile an exhaustive collection of bawdy and profane passages which must have had a good deal to do with the brisk sale of his book. It is well known that both Congreve and Vanbrugh published replies to Collier, and the significant thing is that both of those dramatists accepted Collier's critical position. 'Men', Congreve agreed, 'are to be laugh'd out of their Vices in Comedy...As vicious People are made asham'd of their Follies or Faults, by seeing them expos'd in a ridiculous manner, so are good People at once both warn'd and diverted at their Expence.'[2] 'What I have done', Vanbrugh claimed, 'is in general a discouragement to vice and folly.'[3] The truth is surely different: neither Congreve nor Vanbrugh had given serious thought to discouraging vice (folly is perhaps a different matter) until Collier had put it into their heads; and then, in the same sort of way as M. Jourdain suddenly realised that he had been talking prose for over forty years without knowing it, they discovered that they had been writing satires. Undoubtedly we should have heard much less about the corrective aims of comedy if the comic drama in England had not been under constant attack, and some sort of prestige advertising had not been required to justify it.

There is not much difficulty in distinguishing comedy from satire so long as we stick to theory. It is when we come to consider individual works that the trouble begins. Wycherley's *Plain Dealer* seems to be more satire than comedy, and

The Country Wife more comedy than satire. But which is *The Way of the World*? Again, Meredith calls *The Egoist* a comedy; but many readers would prefer to call it a satire. *Don Juan* must obviously be classed among the satires, but it is also from time to time pure comedy. We must be prepared to find the writer of comedy losing his moral neutrality and slipping into satire, and the satirist occasionally loosening his control over the reader and relaxing into comedy.

Quite apart from comedy, it may sometimes be difficult to tell whether a writer is being satirical or merely recording the facts as he sees them. When we read Halifax's remarkable character of Charles II, we may not find it easy to decide just how satirical the intention is; the level, disenchanted tone, the implied contrast between what kings might be—what indeed some kings have been—and what this very human and imperfect king is, rather suggest satire. But can we be sure? Occasionally, it is true, the satirical intention is quite unmistakable. When Halifax comes to deal with Charles II's amours and mistresses, he opens with a devastating sentence:

It may be said that his Inclinations to Love were the Effects of Health, and a good Constitution, with as little mixture of the *Seraphick* part as ever Man had: And though from that Foundation Men often raise their Passions, I am apt to think his stayed as much as any Man's ever did in the *lower Region*.[1]

We know where we are here; Halifax is inviting us to share in his attitude of fastidious disapproval. But when he goes on to tell us that one of the clues to the character of the King was an 'aversion to bear uneasiness', and that

this made that he had as little Eagerness to oblige, as he had to hurt Men; the Motive of his giving Bounties was rather to make

Men less uneasy to him, than more easy to themselves; and yet no ill-nature all this while. He would slide from an asking Face, and could guess very well. It was throwing a Man off from his Shoulders, that leaned upon them with his whole weight; so that the Party was not gladder to receive, than he was to give.[1]

—when we read this, the air of well-bred indifference with which Halifax sets down the facts may lead us to suppose that the voice we hear is that of the impartial biographer. Yet if we feel (as I dare say most of us do) that his character of Charles II is flecked with satire throughout, we may account for this impression by recalling a remark of Edward Young's that 'historians...may be considered as satirists, and satirists most severe; since such are most human actions, that to relate, is to expose them'.[2] To accept the implications of Young's remark, however, would lead only to critical confusion. If we are to keep our subject in sharp focus we must assume that the satirist always intends to persuade his reader to share his own critical attitude. You cannot be a satirist just by telling the truth; you are a satirist when you consciously compel men to look at what they have tried to ignore, when you wish to destroy their illusions or pretences, when you deliberately tear off the disguise and expose the naked truth.

But here we meet with a complication. The satirist is not the only man who makes us look beneath the surface of things, who compels us to attend to what we have forgotten or have hitherto ignored, who makes us see familiar things in a new and possibly shocking light. It was the peculiar merit of Wordsworth, as Coleridge remarked, to 'awaken the mind's attention from the lethargy of custom', and to make us perceive the significance of incidents and situations in ordinary life 'for which, in consequence of the film of familiarity and selfish solicitude we have eyes, yet see not, ears that hear not, and hearts that neither feel nor understand'.[1] Yet no one hated satire more than Wordsworth did. No poet, too, tried more persistently to penetrate beneath the surface, and, in his own phrase, to see into 'the life of things'. He was, as Coleridge put it, 'a contemplator from whose view...no injuries of wind or weather, or toil, or even of ignorance [could] wholly disguise the human face divine'. It remained legible to *him* 'under the dark lines with which guilt or calamity had cancelled or cross-barred it'.[2] Wordsworth habitually got at the essential in a way which at first sight might seem to resemble that of the satirist—by stripping away the inessential, the varnish, the dirt, the accidental accretions of rank, or fortune, or education. In *The Idiot Boy* he has passed beyond the outward appearance of things (the slobbering child and the fidgety, fussy mother not much wiser than her son) to the essential truth of a human situation: the strange, almost submarine, mental world of the idiot child, and the blinding, overwhelming power of a mother's love for her son. Had we been in Wordsworth's place we might not have felt all this for ourselves; but now that he has revealed it to us we should have little difficulty in seeing what he has seen, and in forgetting what our own more conventional attitude might have led us to see.

Wordsworth, of course, has made acceptance easier by concentrating all his attention on mother and son; we are concerned only with Betty Foy and Johnny. But suppose Johnny had had a sister, a perfectly normal child—the little girl in 'We are Seven' or little Alice Fell—and suppose that

Betty Foy had still lavished all her love on Johnny, and left his sister to look after herself. We have probably all met with, or heard of, that sort of situation: the spastic child to whom almost all the love of the parents is given, while the other children are comparatively neglected. What would our attitude be then? It happens that there is a poem by W. H. Davies, 'The Idiot and the Child', which deals with an almost identical situation.

> There was a house where an old dame
> Lived with a son, his child and wife;
> And with a son of fifty years,
>   An idiot all his life.
>
> When others wept this idiot laughed,
> When others laughed he then would weep:
> The married pair took oath his eyes
>   Did never close in sleep.
>
> Death came that way, and which, think you,
> Fell under that old tyrant's spell?
> He breathed upon that little child
>   Who loved her life so well.
>
> This made the idiot chuckle hard:
> The old dame looked at that child dead
> And him she loved—'Ah well; thank God
>   It is no worse!' she said.[1]

The tone here is manifestly different from that of *The Idiot Boy*: the impact of Davies's far shorter poem is sharper and more immediately startling. The circumstances are not, of course, identical. Here we are presented with a choice to be made between two objects of affection; in *The Idiot Boy* there is only old Susan Gale to compete with Betty Foy's idiot son, and Susan doesn't seem to matter so much, and in any case she has already recovered when Johnny makes his triumphant return. In Davies's poem, therefore, the balance is tipped heavily against any sympathy for the idiot; and yet the old dame can support any loss, however grievous, provided that nothing happens to *him*—an idiot, too, of fifty years' standing. Davies has recorded all this; I do not feel that he is asking us to admire it. But has he passed over into satire? Not quite. And yet he seems to be unwilling to rest on the mere fact; he is certainly struck with the paradox of the situation, and is perhaps verging on overt disapproval. One step further and his poem would be a satire on the old dame for her obsessive preoccupation with the idiot; but Davies has not quite taken that step. Had he intended us to feel that the old woman had completely lost her sense of proportion, even to the extent of becoming heartless, and that she was therefore an object for contempt, or at least for disapproval, he would have made that clear to us, and he would then, by my definition, have been writing satire. As it is, the intention seems to be mixed, and the question therefore remains open.

I cannot now round off this symposium by producing a third poem on the same theme in which the old-dame figure is viewed satirically throughout; but it would not be difficult to envisage such a poem. It would, I imagine, be the work not so much of a callous writer, as of one whose sense of proportion had been outraged, and who was therefore driven to pass judgment where Wordsworth was moved only to a delighted acquiescence, and Davies stopped short with recording a startled observation. The writer of the third poem would necessarily be withholding his sympathy, or at least consciously separating himself from the old dame and viewing her critically. For Wordsworth, who naturally enters into the possession of his experience through sympathy—even, it may be, by almost identifying himself with the object of his contemplation—any such attitude would have been fatal. For him, a poet was at the height of his receptivity when he loved and was happy, when his feelings were vibrating in unison with all living things; by standing apart from the object of his contemplation, critical, hostile, contemptuous, at war with his world, the satirist could never attain to any wholeness of vision. It is significant that, apart from Byron, the English Romantic poets leave satire alone, or else, like Shelley, make very poor work of it.

The Wordsworths and the Tolstoys, with

> an eye made quiet by the power
> Of harmony, and the deep power of joy,

are continually making discoveries; they have their moments of vision, the magnesium flare that suddenly reveals what has lain hidden from our sight. The satirist rarely discovers in this way; he deliberately uncovers what, for one reason or another, has been concealed. What he shows us he has probably known about all the time, and his aim is to show it to us in such a way as to compel our attention. If he has his moments of vision they are concerned with means rather than ends; he discovers, in fact—and often, no doubt, in a sudden flash of understanding—not what he is to say, but how he is to say it, as Swift discovered in the *Modest Proposal* just how he was to bring home to the English what their treatment of the Irish really meant.

What, then, does the satirist see, for he certainly sees something? Not the truth, but one aspect of the truth; not the whole man, but one side of him. He is the advocate pleading a cause, and to secure our agreement he is prepared to ignore much of the evidence and exaggerate the rest. The satirist proceeds characteristically by drastic simplification, by ruthlessly narrowing the area of vision, by leaving out of account the greater part of what must be taken into consideration if we are to realise the totality of a situation or a character. In its extremest form we usually call this process caricature. It is fatal to satire if the reader or spectator should reflect that much might be said on both sides, or that if we knew all we might forgive all. It is, of course, part of the satirist's art to conceal from us that this simplification is taking place, and he does this, as Dryden said of the author of a heroic play, by endeavouring to obtain 'an absolute dominion over the minds of the spectators'.[1] He can obtain this dominion by many different methods: by throwing dust in our eyes, by fascinating us with the verisimilitude of his presentation, by so delighting us with his wit that we never pause to question his argument.

All of those methods were used successfully by Bernard Shaw to induce the English middle classes to reconsider (or more commonly, perhaps, to consider for the first time in their lives) the moral assumptions on which their opinions and conduct were based. The man who makes two grains of sense germinate where only one germinated before deserves well of his countrymen; and if the public has shown itself noticeably uneager to visit the literary shrine at Ayot St Lawrence, we must still be grateful for the brilliance and persistence of Shaw the satirist. Shaw helped to alter the intellectual climate of several generations, and he had a gaiety and charm that are rare enough in the history of satire. But in his endless and delighted exposure of the irrational he is ready to ignore, after the manner of satirists, the true nature of man. Many of the shortcomings that Shaw lays bare with such detached amusement are due to the fact that man is necessarily governed by his emotions as well as by his reason; that he is procreative, that he has to earn his living and cannot afford the time to think everything out, that he has to form habits and make rapid decisions, and so on. When Shaw passes in *Back to Methuselah* from the destructive to the constructive, he gives us those Houyhnhnm-like worthies, the Ancients, calm, passionless, utterly rational, and barely human. We may feel as George II felt when he returned from Hanover to find that in his absence the Queen and Lord Hervey had removed all his favourite pictures and substituted others that he disliked. The King at once gave orders that the missing pictures should be restored to their place; and when Lord Hervey enquired, 'Would your Majesty have the gigantic fat Venus restored too?', the King replied, 'Yes, my Lord; I am not so nice as your Lordship. I like my fat Venus much better than anything you have given me instead of her.'[1] The satirist, of course, is under no obligation to produce a substitute for what he destroys. We must not make the common mistake, too, of assuming that Swift's Houyhnhnms and Shaw's Ancients embody their author's conception of ideal humanity: all that can be fairly deduced from Gulliver's fourth Voyage is that mankind would be a great deal better if it had more of the Houyhnhnm and less of the Yahoo in its make-up.

If the satirist habitually simplifies and exaggerates, if he deals with only one side of a question or one aspect of a man's character—above all, if he is interested only in what he finds and never asks himself how or why it came to be there—must we go on to admit that he is rather a crude person, unaware of the complexity of human life and of human relations? It is true that some famous satirists—Aristophanes, Persius, our own Ben Jonson and Samuel Butler—appear to have had strong but rather obvious minds. They seem to be enormously confident, they have great energy, some of them have an engaging exuberance; but those formidable qualities spring mainly from a robust temperament and plain common sense. Men like Jonson and Butler have little subtlety, and only a limited awareness of what lies beneath the surface of life; they can bring down the obvious follies with both barrels, but the birds have to be large, and preferably of ponderous flight. In stable periods, too, when moral standards are more or less fixed and a code of social behaviour is generally accepted, many lesser men will acquire the confidence which comes from conformity, and will satirise those who straggle from the herd. Such men are not necessarily stupid, but they are rarely minds of the first order. In the eighteenth century they were as common as blackberries, and if many of them are still just readable, it is because the general standard of verse composition was higher in that century than it has ever been since.

Yet there are other satirists—Horace, Erasmus, Swift, Pope, Voltaire, Jane Austen, Flaubert, Shaw, Sir Max Beerbohm—who are anything but crude, and who certainly are not blind to everything but the obvious. The quality of their minds is subtle, their satire is sharp and delicate. As long as they are being satirists, however (and of course some of them are only occasionally satirical), they must accept the limitations that the very nature of satire imposes; and so, whatever they may see at other times, they must close their eyes to what it would be inconvenient for them to take into account. The satirist, like the magistrate on the bench, is there to administer the law, to uphold the order of a civilized community; he brings men and women to the test of certain ethical, intellectual, social, and other standards. In assessing their degree of culpability he may take mitigating circumstances into account, but he is not, as satirist, bound to do so, and if he makes too many allowances he will end by writing something quite other than pure satire. It may be added that he can still be a good satirist even if he fails to live up to his own standards: Dr Johnson's friend, Richard Savage, is not the only man who ever 'mistook the love for the practice of virtue, and was... not so much a good man as the friend of goodness'.[1]

It may now seem that I have given the case for satire away. If the satirist is a sort of literary magistrate laying down the law, who is going to take an interest in him? The case against the satirist may be made to appear worse still if we recall what Walter Pater wrote about the modern mind in his essay on Coleridge. The modern mind, Pater suggested, is distinguished from the ancient 'by its cultivation of the "relative" spirit in place of the "absolute"'. We have become aware of 'a world of fine gradations and subtly linked conditions, shifting intricately as we ourselves change', and as a result we are much less ready to make general observations and confident judgments. 'Hard and abstract moralities', Pater contended, 'are yielding to a more exact estimate of the subtlety and complexity of our life.'[2] If we are to accept Pater's contention, as I think we should, what sort of future remains for the satirist? Who is going to listen to his confident judgments, or have much sympathy with his drastic simplification of the facts?

The answer to those who object to the satirist because he presents them with a partial or grotesque or distorted vision of life is surely the same sort of answer as Sidney gave to those who accused the poets of being liars: the poet 'nothing affirmes, and therefore never lyeth.... Though he recount things not true, yet because hee telleth them not for true he lyeth not.'[1] The satirist, for his part, is putting a case, and to put it effectively he magnifies, diminishes, distorts, cheats: the end with him will always justify the means. Satire is not for the literal-minded. It exists on at least two levels, the overt and the implied; and it can only function properly when the tact and the intelligence and the imagination of the satirist are met by a corresponding response in the reader. The unintelligent either do not read satire at all, or misunderstand its significance when they do. 'The spectrum-analysis of satire', it has been said, 'runs from the red of invective at one end to the violet of the most delicate irony at the other.'[2] To that we may add that the red of invective is now out of fashion, and that twentieth-century satire relies more and more on the indirectness of irony, innuendo, fantasy and fiction of all kinds. The reader has to supply the positive from the satirist's negative, the desirable from the contemptible; he has to interpret the allegory, to understand the significance of the symbol, to realise the implications of what he has read. And to those who feel that the satirical vision is too crude for the delicate analysis of human relationships that we have come to expect in the novel, it may be answered that the ironical contemplation of a Jane Austen or a George Meredith is so detached and precise that it seems rather a judgment passed on the thing observed than a special mode of seeing. The distortion is not in the eye of the beholder, but in the object observed.

What sort of future, then, remains for the satirist? All the indications suggest that today we need him more than ever. As we grow more gregarious, more and more urbanised, we undoubtedly grow sillier, more subject, under the influence of mass-communication and propaganda, to mass hysteria and to the stupidities and vulgarities of a mass culture. Peacock was aware of this tendency at the beginning of the nineteenth century, and Mr Evelyn Waugh in *The Loved One* and elsewhere has satirised some of its contemporary manifestations. As scientific knowledge advances and human life becomes more and more conditioned by applied science, the prospect that man may abdicate his individuality and become a means to an end has alarmed many writers, and Mr Aldous Huxley has offered one satirical warning of a possible future in *Brave New World*. To some extent it might be said that the emphasis in modern satire has shifted from individual man to mankind, and that the satirist is now concerned to save the human race, either from complete extinction, or from a change so fundamental that its essential humanity would be lost. It was such problems, and above all the menace of political totalitarianism, that exercised the mind of George Orwell in his last years, and that found expression in *Animal Farm* and *Nineteen Eighty-Four*. We know much more, or at least we have the means of knowing much more, than our ancestors, but it may be that we are less wise and that we are thinking less. The satirist today is not so much concerned, like Juvenal or Pope, with exposing our moral turpitude as with making us take thought, compelling us to consider where we are heedlessly drifting, urging us to be men and to take charge of our own destinies before it is too late.

Satire, then, is not an extinct dinosaur or pterodactyl, a row of yellow bones in the literary museum, but a living and lively form that has still a vital part to play in twentieth-century literature. If the satirist cannot save us he can at least encourage us not to give up without a struggle; and he can, and does, let in a current of fresh air which fills our lungs and keeps our blood in circulation. And this he does, not because he has lost all hope and belief and is contemplating a waste land with cynical indifference, but because, like Malvolio, he thinks nobly of the human soul.

II

THE PRIMITIVES: INVECTIVE
AND LAMPOON

IT has long been common knowledge that in this and in other European countries the drama grew out of the services of the Church. More recently, a distinguished Cambridge scholar, Dr Owst, has taught us to look for the literary origins of English satire in the writing and preaching of medieval priests and friars.[1] Dr Owst, it may be thought, makes rather too simple an equation between plain denunciation and satire; but he has produced sufficient evidence of a satirical element in medieval preaching to establish his case. So far as they may be called satirists, however, the medieval preachers must be looked upon as a school of primitives, whose work reached some sort of culmination in *The Vision of Piers the Plowman*. Like some other primitives, they painted in hard bright colours, and they leave us in no doubt about what we are to see. I have no right, perhaps, to put *Piers Plowman* among the primitives; but if English satire has its roots in the medieval sermon, it can be said to come into full flower in *Piers Plowman*, and the flower has a strong and unmistakable scent. Such parts of this medieval poem as are satirical—and satire is only one element in a complex and rather bewildering effect—are chiefly in the form of straight-forward denunciation, flavoured at times with a grim humour, and softened to some extent by the dream convention and the allegorical personages.

Our earliest satire, then, is generally marked by direct

denunciation and invective. We must, however, make some distinction between satire and didactic writing in general; the difference is not to be easily defined, but I think we all feel it. Denunciation may pass into satire, but it is not necessarily satirical in itself; it provides one of the possible openings for the satirist, but the preacher may, and most preachers do, refuse to take it. Since definition here is difficult, I shall fall back for the present on examples. In the following passage the rich are being denounced in quite unsparing terms, but I cannot detect the least trace of satire:

How few among the rich have procured their wealth by just measures; how many owe their fortunes to the sins of their parents, how many more to their own! If men's titles were to be tried before a true court of conscience, where false swearing and a thousand vile artifices (that are well known, and can hardly be avoided in human courts of justice), would avail nothing, how many would be ejected with infamy and disgrace? How many grow considerable by breach of trust, by bribery and corruption? how many have sold their religion, with the rights and liberties of themselves and others, for power and employments?[1]

I chose that passage deliberately from a sermon by the greatest of English satirists; but it was not Swift's practice to be satirical in the pulpit. 'Flowers of Rhetoric in Sermons and serious Discourses', he once wrote, 'are like the blue and red Flowers in Corn, pleasing to those who come only for amusement, but prejudicial to him who would reap the Profit from it.'[2] By way of contrast, I take a short passage from another famous preacher, Robert South, where the rich are again mercilessly exposed, but this time with a derisive mockery that is surely satirical:

Let a business of expensive Charity be proposed; and then, as I shew'd before, that in matters of Labour the Lazy Person could find no hands wherewith to *Work*, so neither in this Case can the Religious Miser find any *hands* wherewith *to give*. It is wonderfull to consider, how a command, or call to be Liberal, either upon a Civil or Religious account, all of a sudden impoverishes the Rich, breaks the Merchant, shuts up every private Man's Exchequer, and makes those Men in a minute have nothing at all *to give* who, at the very same instant, want nothing *to spend*. So that instead of relieving the poor, such a command strangely encreases their number, and transforms Rich Men into beggers presently.[1]

South has gone beyond direct denunciation to a humorous mockery of the rich man's meanness; he has accepted with mock solemnity the plea of the well-to-do that they are in financial straits, and cannot make any contribution, and he now reflects with an assumed naïveté on the strange consequences that an appeal to men's charity produces: so far from relieving the poor, it paradoxically increases their numbers. The satirical effect is obtained by make-believe, by South pretending to accept what he doesn't for one moment credit, and so inviting us to join him in a calculated sneer at the expense of the wealthy. South was capable of indignation, and there is something of that in this passage; but he also had a wicked tongue, and a pretty wit, and he enjoyed giving them exercise. If he is still the divine denouncing from the pulpit the meanness of the well-to-do, he is also the artist delighting in the variations that he can play on a promising theme, and on the *reductio ad absurdum* to which his fantasy has led him. He has not lost sight of the thing to be said, but he has passed well beyond the point where it could be said simply and earnestly, and is now playing cat-and-mouse with the idea. It is fun for the preacher, and fun for the congregation; it may conceivably touch the conscience of the rich (in spite of what Swift says) more effectively than plain denunciation. But the essential difference between the two passages is that whereas Swift's mind is entirely concentrated upon his argument, South is sufficiently detatched from his to enjoy the wit and the ironical statement of it. Without such detachment,·we not likely to get satire at all.

Denunciation and invective in one form or another are very frequent in the literature of the fifteenth and sixteenth centuries, and where they rise to satire there is always this element of delight or satisfaction in the writer. We find this self-pleasing extravagance in the work of Dunbar and Skelton, who both have a remarkable talent for name-calling and scurrilous abuse. In 'The Flyting of Dunbar and Kennedy' Dunbar exploits to the full the cacophonous possibilities of Middle Scots and achieves a kind of comic violence that bespatters his opponent with dirt and disgrace.

> Lene larbar, loungeour, bath lowsy in lisk and lonye;
> Fy! skolderit skyn, thow art bot skyre and skrumple;...
> Commirwald crawdoun, na man comptis the ane kers,
> Sueir swappit swanky, swynekeper ay for swaittis.[1]

And so on for 250 lines. 'Poetry should surprise by a fine excess', Keats once wrote. '...It should strike the reader as a wording of his own highest thoughts, and appear almost a remembrance. Its touches of beauty should never be half way, thereby making the reader breathless, instead of content.'[2] If we substitute the word 'ugliness' for 'beauty' and the words 'lowest thoughts' for 'highest thoughts', we come near to understanding the *macabre* effectiveness of Dunbar's invective. I doubt if we really want 250 lines of it, but the effect is necessarily cumulative; one stone flung through one window is good in its way, but a whole volley of stones breaking every window in the building is the natural and desired consummation, and can make a stupendous and unforgettable impression on the mind. Dunbar, of course, is not throwing anything so clean as stones. 'The Flyting of Dunbar and Kennedy' reminds me of nothing so much as the battles we used to fight, when I was a student in Scotland, between the rival parties in a Rectorial election. On those occasions the missiles were rotten eggs, oatmeal, cods' heads, and indeed anything that came to hand. Looking back on it now I can see better what Pope meant when he wrote in the *Dunciad*:

> from Hyperborean skies,
> Embody'd dark, what clouds of Vandals rise.[1]

No doubt it was all quite deplorable, but we were fellow-countrymen of William Dunbar, and it was our simple idea of fun. For it should be remembered that those literary flytings between Dunbar and his contemporaries were good-humoured exercises in denigration, sufficiently well recognised to be included by King James VI in his *Schort Treatise containing some Reulis and Cautelis to be Observit and Eschewit in Scottis Poesie*. Nor are they without parallel in the literature of other European countries. I am told, too, that a form of flyting survives to this day in the University of Uppsala, and similar abusive exercises may linger on in other academic communities.

If only Dunbar and Skelton had belonged to the same generation we might have had a flyting of truly Rabelaisian abundance. Skelton participated in one bout of flyting with Sir Christopher Garnish, and he had a natural talent for abuse that found good material in the Scots, in priests, in

Cardinal Wolsey, and in much else. His buoyant and colloquial manner comes out well in his rapid taunting of the Scots who had campaigned ingloriously under the Duke of Albany:

> Twyt, Scot, yet agayne ones
> We shall breke thy bones,
> And hang you upon polles,
> And byrne you all to colles;
> With twyt, Scot, twyt, Scot, twyt,
> Walke, Scot, go begge a byt
> Of brede at ylke mannes hecke:
> The fynde, Scot, breke thy necke!
> Twyt, Scot, agayne I saye,
> Twyt, Scot, of Galaway,
> Twyt, Scot, shakke thy dogge, hay!
> Twyt, Scot, thou ran away...[1]

This is the voice of the schoolboy shouting out insults to the townees from behind the school railings, a verbal pummelling from a safe distance. As with Dunbar's vituperation, the effect depends largely upon the sound; and the sounds here—

> With twyt, Scot, twyt, Scot, twyt,
> Walke, Scot, go begge a byt—

might almost come from some raucous and voluble parrot in his cage. As with Dunbar again, the secret lies partly in the amplitude of the abuse, in keeping it up so long, in simply holding the floor; the abuse pours out in a torrent, sweeping the derided object away with it and submerging all distinction. It is, of course, mainly a matter of vocabulary with Skelton, but the rapid tumbling metre and the clattering rhyme reinforce the ribald effect. Like the author of *Hudibras*, too, Skelton makes effective use of a debasing imagery, drawn often from the less endearing animals:

28

> Yet ye dare do nothynge,
> But lepe away lyke frogges,
> And hyde you under logges,
> Lyke pygges and lyke hogges,
> And lyke maungy dogges.[1]

Behind it all sits Skelton, enjoying himself enormously, and filling the air with a grotesque harmony.

> His virtues walk'd their narrow round,
> Nor made a pause, nor left a void;
> And sure the Eternal Master found
> The single talent well employ'd.

Skelton comes nearer to true satire in his *Colin Clout*, where, by putting into the mouth of the simple Colin what men are saying, he achieves a devastating report on the state of the nation. *Why Come ye not to Court?* is a remarkably brave indictment of Cardinal Wolsey, but to call it satire would be to stretch the term further than it will go.

Near the close of *Why Come ye not to Court?* Skelton informs us that he has written the poem at Juvenal's request. 'Blame Iuvenall,' he says, 'blame not me.' Skelton was a classical scholar, but his spontaneous abuse is very far from the controlled art of Juvenal. It was not until the close of the sixteenth century that English poets began to imitate the Roman satirists seriously, and when they did the results were not particularly happy. The first complete translation of Juvenal to be published in English was that of Sir Robert Stapleton in 1647; but a translation by Barton Holyday was made some time before that, though not published till 1673. Persius had been translated in 1617 by Holyday, and Thomas Drant's translation of Horace had appeared fifty years earlier, in 1567. That Persius should have been englished before Juvenal is on the face of it rather odd; but the reason is not so much that there was less of Persius to translate as that Isaac Casaubon's learned edition had appeared in 1605, with an essay explaining the nature of classical satire. Persius, too, would undoubtedly appeal to that neo-stoicism in which a number of Elizabethan authors showed so marked an interest. At all events, Juvenal and Persius exercised a rather malign influence over the young Elizabethan poets, John Donne, Joseph Hall, John Marston, and Everard Guilpin, who in the last decade of the sixteenth century took to writing formal satires in what they believed to be the high Roman fashion. In almost every way the Elizabethan age was thoroughly un-Roman. It might prove hard to justify this statement in a few words; yet we cannot help being conscious of a naïveté and an unashamed enthusiasm in Elizabethan England, a willingness to be stirred by great events and great men that is far removed from the materialism and sophistication of, at any rate, imperial Rome. Even in their vices the Elizabethans had usually a kind of innocence; and though London was a metropolitan city of wealth and poverty, with a thriving underworld of taverns and brothels, of crooks and bullies, the fresh air of an essentially rural economy still kept the moral atmosphere clean. The classical historians assure us that the age of Nero and Domitian was really as bad as Juvenal painted it, and that to get an adequate parallel in modern times we must go to the short and tyrannical reigns of Mussolini and Hitler. But Elizabethan London was not of that order at all. There is always, no doubt, a sufficiency of vice and folly at any period, and in any large city; the satirist need never go short of material. He ought, however, to content himself with the

crimes of his own day and his own country, and not import
them from foreign countries and past ages. There is, in fact,
an air of assumed indignation in the Elizabethan imitators of
Juvenal and Persius; they pull terrible faces, and denounce
vices that either do not exist in their country at all or that are
very far from being general. They were all young men, too,
in their early twenties, when they wrote their satires, and it
is hard to believe that they had much first-hand knowledge
of the flaming sins that they denounced so tremendously.

They were, of course, only doing what they thought satire
demanded. They had been taught by Thomas Drant, in a
poem prefixed to his collection of satires, *A Medicinable
Morall* (1566), that

> Satyre is a tarte and carpyng kynd of verse,
> An instrument to pynche the prankes of men,

and that

> those that wyll them write,
> With taunting gyrds and glikes and gibes must vexe
> the lewde,
> Strayne curtesy, ne reck of mortall spyte.[1]

That was the normal Tudor idea of satire. To Puttenham it
seemed that the satirist should 'taxe the common abuses and
vice of the people in rough and bitter speaches', and he
refers his readers to 'Lucilius, Juvenall, and Persius among
the Latines, and with us he that wrote the booke called
Piers plowman'.[2] (Horace is cited among the lyrical poets.)
It comes therefore as a surprise to find Sir John Harington
declaring in 1591 that satire is 'wholly occupied in mannerly
and covertly reproving of all vices';[3] but Harington on this
occasion was engaged in defending poetry from the charge
of scurrility and lewdness, and was borrowing most of his

arguments from Sir Philip Sidney, who apparently thought of Horace rather than of Juvenal when he came to the defence of satire. The more usual Elizabethan idea of satire is to be found in such misanthropic characters as Shakespeare's Thersites and Apemantus who rail and snarl so bitterly in the contemporary drama; rough-tongued, honest, sardonic fellows who mouth their 'taunting gyrds, and glikes and gibes' with all the appearance, to use a modern colloquialism, of 'putting on an act'. The type survives in Restoration drama in such plays as Wycherley's *The Plain Dealer*. The false derivation of the word 'satire' from the rough and hairy satyr of Greek mythology undoubtedly had much to do with the belief that satire must be rugged and abrupt and violent. Ruggedness was partly a matter of language, but it could also be attained by metrical irregularity, and Donne and Marston, at least, freely availed themselves of this opportunity.

Unfortunately the Elizabethan satirists made yet another assumption—that satire should be obscure. No doubt Juvenal and Persius, and Persius especially, were to blame again. Hall, at any rate, was convinced that it was of the nature of satire not only to be 'harsh of stile', but also to be 'hard of conceipt'.[1] In the prologue to book III of his *Virgidemiae* he takes note of the fact that some readers have criticised his satires for not being obscure enough—

> Not, ridle-like, obscuring their intent:
> But packe-staffe plaine uttring what thing they ment.[2]

In the first satire of book IV Hall proceeds to show that he can rise above mere perspicuity. Here, indeed, he manages to write almost as badly as Marston; but it must have been uphill work, for Hall was obviously a sensible person with a prejudice in favour of being understood, and before long he lapses into the intelligible. Hall, in fact, is much nearer to Pope than either Donne or Marston. In Donne's satires the reader goes staggering from one couplet to another, coming up against unexpected objects in the half-darkness and never really sure where the poet is taking him. In Hall the verse runs more easily (and ease without too great facility is an advantage in verse satire), and it often builds up into passages which have taken shape in his mind.

The verse satirists we have been considering were not obscure enough to escape the eye and the understanding of authority. In the summer of 1599 Whitgift, Archbishop of Canterbury, and Bancroft, Bishop of London, ordered the satires of Hall, Marston and Guilpin to be publicly burnt (Donne's, of course, were not yet in print), and issued an edict 'That no Satyres or Epigrams be printed hereafter'. It seems to have made very little difference. In the year following the edict Samuel Rowlands published *The Letting of Humour's Blood in the Head-vein*, and volumes of satires and epigrams continued to appear at frequent intervals. In the epigrams the influence of Martial is naturally predominant.

I turn now from verse to prose. Nothing, perhaps, is so thoroughly dead as the ecclesiastical controversies of the past, and the modern reader will not easily be persuaded that the once famous Martin Marprelate tracts are worth reading. It is true that their audacities will no longer quicken a single pulse-beat, and that most of us view the controversy between the Bishops and the Puritans with all the impartiality of boredom. If we appreciate Martin's sardonic pleasantries at all, it can only be at a long remove from the issues that once gave most of them their life and vigour. With much of the satirical writing of past centuries we are inevitably in the position of someone who sees the joke, but is not moved to laugh at it. Those satirical strokes that were 'wont to set the table on a roar' are fortunate if they now provoke a learned smile; at best, like Coleridge looking at the stars gliding between the dark clouds, 'we see, not feel, how beautiful they are'. Yet Martin Marprelate, whoever he may have been, has still some claim upon our attention; not because he is, like Junius, one of the great unknowns of English satire, but because he had evolved a technique of denigration that is characteristically English, or, at least, unmistakably Cockney, and because his irrepressible self-confidence still comes over to us across the centuries with the sound of living speech. Martin is an adept at calling names. Bishop Aylmer is referred to as 'Dumb John of London', and Whitgift is variously 'Master Whitgift', 'John of Canterbury', 'John Cant', 'Your Canturburiness', 'His Gracelessness of Cant', and 'the Pope of Lambeth'. It is all, no doubt, very like the street urchin chalking scurrilities on walls; but it had a good satirical *raison d'être*. The bishops were entrenched in their great palaces, and rode abroad with a hundred or more retainers in livery; and for the Puritan Martin what was needed was that they should be brought down to the level of the rank-and-file Christian. Martin's familiar, cheeky, chatty manner robbed the bishops of their ecclesiastical dignity and took away the terrors of their office; it also endeared him to the common reader, who must often, as Martin himself points out, have boggled at the elaborate periods of episcopal prose. In the epitome to his first tract he is replying to an elaborate defence of ecclesiastical government put forth by Dean

Bridges of Salisbury, running to over 1400 pages quarto. He breaks off to deal, in passing, with the Bishop of London, and then returns to the long-suffering Bridges:

> But now alas, alas, Brother Bridges, I had forgotten you all this while. My brother London and I were so busy, that we scarce thought of you. Why could you not put me in mind that you stayed all the while? But it is no matter, we will make the quicker despatch of your business.[1]

There is no answer to such perky insolence except to run the man out of the room; but this the bishops could never do, for they did not know who he was, and consequently could never lay hands on him. It is, at any rate, with such easy effrontery that Martin Marprelate deflates the pride of prelates. If he is not a great name in the history of satire, he is unquestionably a master in the art of denigration.

In the Edict of 1599 it was ordered 'that all Nasshes bookes and Doctor Harvyes bookes be taken wheresoever they maye be found and that none of theire bookes be ever printed hereafter'. Thomas Nashe, I suppose, may be looked upon as a disturber of the peace; but compared with the strictly practical satire of Marprelate the exuberant vituperation of Nashe sounds like the clashing of cymbals in a hollow cave. We can agree with Professor C. S. Lewis that 'an enemy to bespatter was clearly an artistic necessity to one who had just discovered a style so suited to invective'.[2] Nashe's satire exists in a vacuum. His attitude to controversy is like that of the Irishman who asked, 'Is this a private fight, or can anyone join in?' But the very virtuosity of Nashe should serve to remind us again that one constant element in satire (however much the satirist may play it down or try to conceal it) is the pleasure he derives from his technical skill—from pulling out the satirical stops in the organ, and letting its snarling pipes vibrate with harmonious or cacophonous invective. Swift, who was unusually honest in examining his own motives, was ready to admit that one good reason for writing satire is 'the private satisfaction and pleasure of the writer'.[1] This pleasure may derive, as it clearly does with Nashe, from a natural talent for abuse, or it may be adulterated with every degree of malice, spleen, and self-righteousness. It was self-righteousness that Oscar Wilde had in mind when he made one of his characters remark in *The Importance of being Earnest*, 'On an occasion of this kind it becomes more than a moral duty to speak one's mind. It becomes a pleasure.'[2] When someone says, 'I told him exactly what I thought of him', we may perhaps question whether 'exactly' is quite the right word to describe what was actually said, but we have no difficulty in recognising the satisfaction of the speaker. Without this element of self-satisfaction satire would lose most of its gaiety, and that recklessness which usually leads to its most imaginative effects.

In the seventeenth century, as we should expect—that century in which men took sides with such passionate conviction—we meet with many formidable writers of invective. There is John Cleveland, who is probably known to the general reader of today by a solitary couplet in *The Rebel Scot*. But let us take it in its context, where it is even better. The Scots had come to the aid of the English Parliament, and had invaded England. Ireland, says Cleveland, can no longer boast that she has no snakes ('fosters no venom') since the Scotch plantation; and as for England, she can no longer

> her feigned antiquity maintain;
> Since they came in, England hath wolves again.

From England the poet now turns to a sardonic contemplation of the country from which the Scots have issued:

> He that saw Hell in's melancholy dream
> And in the twilight of his fancy's theme,
> Scared from his sins, repented in a fright,
> Had he viewed Scotland, had turned proselyte.
> A land where one may pray with cursed intent,
> 'Oh may they never suffer banishment!'
> Had Cain been Scot, God would have changed his doom;
> Not forced him wander but confined him home![1]

That passage is effective partly because it *is* a passage; it gathers strength as it proceeds until it finally reaches the couplet that everyone remembers. Cleveland, of course, aimed in his writing at the wit of the Metaphysicals. The trouble with the Metaphysical style of writing for the purposes of satire is that it tends to scatter the satirist's punches. Cleveland's wit usually goes skipping from one thought to another, and though the individual jabs and thrusts are often effective they are rarely followed up. When Dryden, on the other hand, has finished with Shaftesbury or Buckingham, they are down on the floor for a count of ten.

Cleveland's satire seems to owe little or nothing to Juvenal; it belongs to the native English tradition. With John Oldham, however, the influence of Juvenal is unmistakable, and even earned for him the title of 'the English Juvenal'. Besides his two free and intelligent imitations of Juvenal's third and thirteenth satires, there are fairly frequent echoes of the Roman satirist in his poetry, and his *Satires upon the Jesuits* have the uncompromising denunciation we associate

37

with Juvenal. Oldham survives in *The Oxford Book of Quotations* by only two lines. This may seem to be a rather primitive test; but it is, after all, a relevant one, for we do expect a writer of verse satire not merely to have memorable things to say, but to say them in such a way that we shall never forget them. Oldham was much read in his own day; but his effectiveness depended to a large extent on political and religious passions which had only to be touched, like an exposed nerve, to produce an immediate reaction. We have our own exposed nerves in the twentieth century; but the religious one appears to be deadened, and our political troubles are of a very different order from those of Restoration England.

In any survey of political satire we must at least look at Andrew Marvell. The reputation of Marvell is probably higher today than it has ever been, but not on account of his satires, which represent about half of what he wrote in verse. The little two-volume edition in the 'Muses' Library' rather pointedly labels volume I 'Poems' and volume II 'Satires'. The satires certainly have wit, and even after a lapse of nearly three hundred years the outspokenness (and, it must be added, the indecency) of such poems as the *Instructions to a Painter* or the *Dialogue between two Horses* still have the power to startle us. The outspokenness and the indecency, and to a lesser extent the wit, also appear in much of the verse collected in the various volumes of *Poems on Affairs of State*, for this was one of the golden periods of English invective. Here and there attack rises above mere invective, as in a satirical poem that has been attributed, wrongly perhaps, to Marvell. The writer leads off with a description of Charles II, and in the fourth line contrives a shattering

comment on Clarendon and the other royalists who followed
the young King into exile:

> Of a tall Stature, and of sable hue,
> Much like the Son of Kish that lofty Jew,
> Twelve Years compleat he suffer'd in Exile
> And kept his Father's Asses all the while.[1]

The wit and the audacity there are good enough for Marvell,
or Rochester, or Dryden, but the rest of the poem gives us
the audacity without the wit. What distinguishes Marvell
from the many anonymous scribblers of the period is a mind
constantly at work, the freshness and unexpectedness of his
imagery, and the imaginative extravagance of his humour;
even in this rough, hard-hitting stuff the poet of 'Appleton
House' and 'The Garden' shines through. An exception,
too, can be made of Rochester in such poems as 'The
Maim'd Debauchee' and 'A Satire against Mankind', but
much of his satirical verse is impromptu, rambling, hit-or-
miss stuff.

Unrelieved invective soon grows monotonous. It becomes
much more amusing—and this is true of satire in general—
when the satirist discovers some mould or form which will
give his satirical ideas an effective shape. No one has yet
written a History of Satirical Forms, but it would be something well worth having. In the Restoration period a considerable number of those forms were developed, and used
again and again. One of them was 'Instructions to a Painter'.
On 3 June 1665 the Duke of York obtained a victory over
the Dutch fleet, and shortly afterwards the courtly Waller
published a poem in praise of the Duke, entitled *Instructions
to a Painter, for the Drawing of the Posture and Progress of
His Majesties Forces at Sea, under the Command of His Royal*

Highness.... Waller was tempting providence. That same summer of 1665 saw the outbreak of the Great Plague, followed next year by the Great Fire; and on 3 June 1666, the anniversary of the Duke of York's victory, Monck was defeated in a four-day battle at sea, which began off Ostend and finished up off the Downs. Worse was to follow. Most of the money voted by parliament for the maintenance of the fleet had been appropriated by the King for purposes more closely connected with love than war; and in June 1667 the Dutch under the command of de Ruyter sailed unmolested up the Thames and burnt a large part of the English fleet in the Medway. Shortly after the publication of Waller's poem, there appeared a satirical *Second Advice to a Painter*; and other Advices, Instructions, or Directions to a Painter kept coming from the press at short intervals. Marvell certainly contributed a 'Last Instructions' and a 'Further Advice' to the series, but had probably no hand in the rest. Among other satirical moulds popular at this time there were the 'Sessions of the Poets' (used for literary satire), 'Auctions of Pictures' (mainly for the purposes of lampoon), parodies of the Bible (and of course satires like *Absalom and Achitophel* with a biblical framework), mock advertisements, fables, 'Trips', 'Spys', 'News from the Dead', and many more.

Poems like the *Instructions to a Painter* or Oldham's *Satires on the Jesuits* or *Absalom and Achitophel* are the forest trees of Restoration satire. Beneath them lies a thick undergrowth of lampoons and libels. Charles II and the royal mistresses were obvious targets, but so were the Duke of York, Shaftesbury, the Hon. Edward Howard, Sir Carr Scroope, and so on down to those too obscure to be any longer identifiable. No one was safe from the anonymous libeller. 'Women's Reputations,' we are told by a contemporary observer, 'of what Quality or Conduct soever, have been reckon'd as lawful Game as Watchmen's Heads; and 'tis thought as glorious a piece of Gallantry by some of our modern Sparks to libel a Woman of Honour, as to kill a Constable who is doing his duty.'[1] What was too slanderous or too indecent, even by Restoration standards, to be printed, could be circulated in manuscript; and a certain 'Captain' Robert Julian, known as Secretary to the Muses, ran a profitable black market in manuscript lampoons which he picked up and sold at the coffee houses and elsewhere. It would probably be a mistake to attribute many of those Restoration epigrams and lampoons to the influence of Martial, although several selections from his epigrams in English were published during the period, and the Latin text went through a number of editions. The Restoration lampoon is rather a natural product of the gregarious, leisured, scandalous and scandal-loving world of Restoration society; it was an obvious mode of expression for the mob of gentlemen and others who wrote with ease, and, if they were lucky, with some semblance of wit. A literary genre which was cultivated by such men as Rochester and Sedley could hardly fail to produce some writing of distinction; but if we try to imagine the public for whom those Restoration lampoons and libels were written, we may be reminded of Pope's Cloacina in the *Dunciad*,

> List'ning delighted to the jest unclean
> Of link-boys vile, and watermen obscene.[2]

There remains to be mentioned one famous name of the Restoration period, the author of *Hudibras*. It may seem perverse to classify him among the primitives, and to discuss him along with writers who are mainly distinguished by their talent for abuse. Samuel Butler has himself so well in hand, his contempt is so good-humoured, the range of his mind is so considerable, and his wit is at times so close to that of the Metaphysical poets, that I may seem to be doing him less than justice by considering him in this context. But so far as satire is concerned, I think he must stay among the primitives—the greatest of them all, no doubt, but essentially a master of denigration rather than of developed satire. We have now looked at enough examples to see why writers who confine themselves to invective and lampoon can hardly be regarded as satirists in the fullest sense. They are almost purely negative and destructive; no positive values emerge from their denigration and abuse. We can see well enough that Skelton and Cleveland do not like the Scots, just as other people do not like the Jews, or the Germans, or the English, but they offer us nothing better in their place. Behind the satire of Juvenal and Swift and Pope, of Voltaire and Shaw, there lies some vision of the good life, of order and decency, of good sense and modera-tion, of intelligence and spiritual alertness. It would not be quite true to say that no positive values emerge from Butler's *Hudibras*, but he is so set on bethumping his victims that we are conscious of little else than the dust and the clatter.

Butler's method in *Hudibras* is not quite uniform. There are one or two passages of mock-heroic, and many more in which he is simply calling a spade a spade; but his prevalent method is that of burlesque, and burlesque ('making Dido talk like a fishwife') aims at ridicule by way of diminishing and travesty. The economic, political, and religious issues which divided England during the Civil War, and which then seemed so important that men like Pym and Hampden and Milton on the one side, and Clarendon and Viscount Falkland on the other, were ready to fight, and if necessary to die, for them, are subjected in the opening lines of *Hudibras* to this levelling and diminishing process:

> When civil fury first grew high,
> And men fell out, they knew not why;
> When hard words, jealousies, and fears,
> Set folks together by the ears,
> And made them fight, like mad or drunk,
> For Dame Religion, as for punk....

We know at once where we are; and for the rest of this long poem we continue to have the same worm's eye view of public events and intellectual controversies.

Burlesque has its own special virtues: it enables a satirist to strike with great force and confidence, and it leaves us in no doubt about what we are meant to think. But an extended burlesque like *Hudibras* carries with it the danger of monotony, and of a resulting boredom. This danger, it may be argued, is implicit in every satirical work of any considerable length; the satirist erects an elaborate pretence, and in time we have had enough, and want a change. But the writer of burlesque, because he keeps harping on the same extravagant note, is especially open to the charge of monotony, and Butler certainly does not escape it. And there is still a more serious objection to burlesque as a satirical technique. It is too indiscriminate. It acts like the mud splashed up by a passing lorry on the faces and stockings of the passers-by, falling alike on the just and the unjust. Or, to use a simile that might have appealed to Butler, it acts like grape-shot or chain-shot, wounding and shattering over a wide and un-defined area; whereas true satire is aimed at an object, and hits it with a single bullet.

Butler, it would appear, was a man who was in some degree at war with himself, and who therefore leaves on the mind a sense of quite unusual talents not fully employed. The late Professor W. P. Ker pointed out one of the strange contra-dictions in him: he is up to date in his thinking, and indeed anticipates in some ways the eighteenth-century view of life, and at the same time he is out of date and old-fashioned in his manner and style. 'The bottles are old,' as Ker puts it, 'but the wine is new. It was Butler's defect or his misfortune that he never found any perfectly adequate form of expres-sion for what he had in mind.'[1] Those who think that *Hudibras* is the adequate expression of all that Butler had to say should turn to the remarkable jottings in his *Notebooks* or to his *Characters*, where they will find abundant evidence of a singularly discriminating mind. It is probably useless to speculate on what drove Butler to write burlesque. He writes it so well, and the clodhopping rhythm and grotesque imagery are so obviously an essential part of him, that it would be wrong to suggest he was merely following the burlesque fashion established by Paul Scarron in France. A predilection for burlesque is often a marked feature of the satirical temperament; it may be found in the insensitive, but it is sometimes, surprisingly enough, to be met with in writers of great delicacy. A contemporary of Butler's, Charles Cotton, was at once a lyrical poet of sensitive feeling and the author of a coarse and boisterous travesty of Virgil. When we meet with a poster in a London Underground station in which a moustache has been added to the face of some brightly smiling girl, we have the same sort of mentality at work as produced Cotton's *Virgil Travestie*. Cotton undoubtedly admired the *Aeneid*, and yet he could scrawl his smutty caricatures all over it. There is evidence here, not perhaps of a split personality, but of a divided mind.

Invective did not die with the seventeenth century. In Dr Arbuthnot's grim epitaph on the unspeakable Colonel Francis Charteris it is running as strongly as ever; and in Charles Churchill's lines on Bishop Warburton, who

> was so proud, that should he meet
> The Twelve Apostles in the street,
> He'd turn his nose up at them all,
> And shove his Saviour from the wall....[1]

we cannot complain of any want of vigour. And, still in the eighteenth century, we have what is to my mind one of the greatest of all invective poems, 'Holy Willie's Prayer', by Robert Burns.

In the nineteenth century the tone becomes noticeably more restrained; but, given the necessary provocation, a Tennyson was capable of falling like a hawk on Richard Monckton Milnes,[2] and a Browning of addressing some bitter verses to the dead Edward FitzGerald, who had sneered at the death of Elizabeth Barrett Browning,[3] and a visit of Samuel Butler to Canada produced the memorable 'O God! O Montreal!' In the present century Belloc and Chesterton were both masters of a fine scorn, which was directed, with considerable fortitude and with varying degrees of justification, against some of their prominent contemporaries. Yeats, too, once opened in a fine blaze of indignation in his lines 'To a Wealthy Man who promised

a second subscription to the Dublin Municipal Gallery if it
were proved the People wanted Pictures':

> You gave, but will not give again
> Until enough of Paudeen's pence
> By Biddy's halfpennies have lain
> To be 'some sort of evidence'. . . .[1]

Statesmen and politicians, too, have continued to contribute their distinguished quota to the literature of invective.
The first Earl Baldwin's retort to certain sections of the
British press, 'The Press has power without responsibility—
the privilege of harlots throughout the ages', will not soon be
forgotten; and in more recent times Sir Winston Churchill
has castigated some of his country's enemies in memorable
invective, all the more telling because it suddenly interrupted with a colloquial, if calculated, directness the more
classical rhythms of his great speeches. Invective on an
extended scale, or invective as a satirical maid-of-all-work is
no longer in fashion; but given the hour, and the man, and
the consenting audience, it can still be as shattering as ever.

III

VERSE SATIRE

IF Juvenal had continued to dominate English satire as he dominated the work of men like Marston and Oldham, I should have had a different, and a duller story to tell. Oldham's *Satires upon the Jesuits* blaze like a bonfire in a dark and windy night. They are therefore not negligible, but a succession of such bonfires would soon cease to have much effect. *Saeva indignatio* is very well in its way, but the more *saeva* the *indignatio*, the more a satirist must bring to his work a fine control, and men like Oldham give one the impression of being carried along on a horse that has bolted, and even at times of encouraging the horse to bolt when its impetuosity shows signs of flagging.

Scholars will no doubt continue to argue about the sincerity of Juvenal. If anyone supposes that no satirist can be deeply concerned about the evils he is denouncing and at the same time enjoy the denunciation, then I think he must deny sincerity to Juvenal. But surely a satirist can hate the evil thing, and enjoy his own power to express it. What, at any rate, seems to distinguish Juvenal, and what has kept him alive, is the far from common combination of strong feeling with the highest qualities of style. The feeling may be largely generated by the act of composition, but it must have felt like genuine feeling to Juvenal while he was composing his satires. What at least is not in doubt is that with him feeling did not lead to wild and whirling words, but to a more and more deadly precision, a devastating finality of expression which leaves no more to be said. So we have the feeble and diseased old man of the tenth satire whose body is now warmed only by a fever,[1] or the townsman in the third satire who buys a tiny estate in the country and becomes 'lord of a single lizard'.[2] It is such sardonic felicities of thought and expression that Juvenal's English imitators could so rarely achieve; too often they give us only the invective without the wit, the stateliness without that grim gaiety that Dr Johnson noted in the Roman satirist.[3]

It is therefore of some importance in the history of English verse satire that although Juvenal remained a great name all through the neo-classical period, and was imitated with varying success by such writers as Samuel Johnson, other ancient satirists (notably Horace, and also Lucian) began to receive more attention, and English satire was no longer confined to the narrow and turbulent channel of Juvenalian invective. It is true that our first great verse satirist, Dryden, gives the preference to Juvenal over all the rest, but he only arrives at this judgment after a prolonged consideration of the rival merits of Persius and Horace.[4] In the end, he is prepared to 'let Juvenal ride first in triumph', but Horace, who comes second, is 'but *just* the second'. What Dryden admired in Juvenal was his ability to 'declaim ...wittily and sharply'; but he was equally convinced that 'the nicest and most delicate touches of satire consist in fine raillery',[5] and in that Horace had no superior. Dryden's own satire contains both invective and raillery; and if I say that he was more influenced by Juvenal than by Horace, it is because the raillery appears to have come naturally to him, whereas the declamatory manner was one that he had to assume for the purpose of his satire, and there he did require a master.

The poem in which Dryden comes nearest to Juvenal is not *MacFlecknoe* nor *Absalom and Achitophel*, but *The Medal*. *The Medal* appeared four months after *Absalom and Achitophel*, and in the interval Dryden's attitude to Shaftesbury and to the crisis he had precipitated underwent a significant change. The very circumstance of the medal which was struck by the triumphant Whigs to commemorate the occasion when a London Grand Jury rejected the bill indicting Shaftesbury for high treason is one that might well have appealed to Juvenal. Dryden, at any rate, begins by exploiting such ludicrous possibilities as attach to anyone sitting for his portrait, and then quickly proceeds to an unqualified denunciation of the sitter.

> Five daies he sate for every cast and look;
> Four more than God to finish Adam took.
> But who can tell what Essence angels are
> Or how long Heav'n was making Lucifer?
> Oh, cou'd the Style that copy'd every grace
> And plough'd such furrows for an Eunuch face,
> Cou'd it have formed his ever-changing Will,
> The various Piece had tir'd the Graver's Skill!
> A Martial Heroe first, with early care
> Blown, like a Pigmee by the Winds, to war.
> A beardless Chief, a Rebel e'er a Man,
> (So young his hatred to his Prince began.)
> Next this, (how wildly will Ambition steer!)
> A Vermin wriggling in th' Usurper's ear,
> Bart'ring his venal wit for sums of gold,
> He cast himself into the Saint-like mould;
> Groan'd, sigh'd, and pray'd, while Godliness was gain,
> The lowest Bag-pipe of the Squeaking train.[1]

This appalling succession of blows, ruthlessly hammered home to left and right, and delivered so rapidly that the victim has no time to recover from the first before the second falls, is surely characteristic of Juvenal. It may be thought that the style is too low for the Roman satirist; but if Juvenal is less colloquial than Horace he is not all stateliness, and is not afraid of the low word on occasion. There is, too, a contemptuous wit in Dryden's lines that Juvenal would have appreciated. At all events, *The Medal* differs from the other major satires of Dryden by consisting of almost continuous denunciation; it is a good deal more outspoken than *Absalom and Achitophel*, and the portrait of Shaftesbury, unlike that of the earlier poem, has no redeeming features at all. The situation had worsened considerably since Dryden first attacked Shaftesbury. In *The Medal* he seems to be an angry man, and it is possible that he is angry because he is alarmed. Dryden's charge against Shaftesbury is that he has 'cut down the banks that made the bar',[1] and the seas of popular rebellion are now flooding through the breach. Like Matthew Arnold two centuries later, Dryden was nervous of mob rule, and the bitterness of his attack on Shaftesbury is the measure of his anxiety. There were, he held, only two valid reasons for personal satire: the first was in revenge for some affront, and the second was when a man 'is become a public nuisance'.[2] In Dryden's eyes Shaftesbury must have seemed worse even than that; he had become a public menace. But, if a story handed down by Spence is true, Dryden's outspokenness in *The Medal* may also be due to the fact that the satire was commissioned by the King. 'One day', according to Spence, 'as the King was walking in the Mall, and talking with Dryden, he said, " If I were a poet, and I think I am poor enough to be one, I would write a poem on such a subject, in the following manner";

and then gave him the plan for it.'[1] It is true that 'If I were a poet, and I think I am poor enough to be one' sounds very like an authentic utterance of Charles II; but the anecdote would be more plausible if it referred to *Absalom and Achitophel*, which the King is also said to have suggested to Dryden, and which certainly has a plan, whereas *The Medal* has nothing to do with Shaftesbury's medal after the first few lines, and develops from that point into an unambiguous denunciation of Shaftesbury and the Whigs. At all events, Dryden could be quite sure that his poem would be acceptable to the King, and that may help to account for the unmeasured, and on the whole uncharacteristic, invective of *The Medal*.

Absalom and Achitophel, a much longer poem, has far more variety of tone and, though Dryden's purpose is serious, there is little of the angry satire of *The Medal*. When the poem was published, in November 1681, Shaftesbury had been lying for some months in the Tower facing a charge of high treason, the Exclusion Bill had been thrown out at the second reading, and the King had dissolved parliament. In those circumstances Dryden may well have believed that the country was not likely to be troubled with Shaftesbury much longer, and that in writing *Absalom and Achitophel* he was merely giving the *coup de grâce* to a beaten enemy and a lost cause. If he really thought that the worst was over—and in the summer of 1681 the odds appeared to be all against Shaftesbury and the supporters of the Duke of Monmouth—this would account for the tone of easy contempt (so different from that of *The Medal*) in which at least large sections of the poem are written.

Dryden set about the writing of *Absalom and Achitophel*,

his first long poem for fourteen years, after a prolonged spell of writing plays. In composing the speeches for Achitophel, Absalom and David he had not moved very far from the position of the dramatist who puts arguments of one sort or another into the mouths of his characters. The dramatist does not need to be personally involved in the issues of the debate; indeed, he had better not be. The main difference between Dryden the dramatist and Dryden the author of *Absalom and Achitophel* is that in the poem he has been retained by the Crown, and entrusted with the case for the prosecution. Fortunately for Dryden it happens to be a case which it is a pleasure for him to put; and though he also states the position of Shaftesbury and his friends in words that certainly do not travesty the arguments of the Exclusionists, he takes care that the Whig dogs shall get the worst of it. But there is no question of his heart bleeding for his poor country. Not, at any rate, in *Absalom and Achitophel*; it may be bleeding a little in *The Medal*. In *Absalom and Achitophel* his attitude was just right for satire; he cared enough to put the issues firmly and incisively but not so much as to be in any danger of losing his balance. Since he was not too deeply engaged, he had leisure to be witty, and to introduce, in the characters of Zimri and even Achitophel, that fine raillery in which he himself considered that 'the nicest and most delicate touches of satire' are to be found.

It is in this poem, too, that the satirical possibilities of the heroic couplet are fully revealed for the first time. When Dryden exposes the stinginess of Slingsby Bethel by telling us that

> His Cooks, with long disuse, their Trade forgot;
> Cool was his Kitchin, though his Brains were hot...[1]

he is very far indeed from what Jack Ketch's wife called 'a plain piece of work, a bare hanging'.[1] When he writes more grimly of Shaftesbury that he is

> For close Designs and crooked Counsels fit,
> Sagacious, Bold, and Turbulent of wit...
> In Friendship false, implacable in Hate,
> Resolv'd to Ruine or to Rule the State...[2]

the cadence, the alliteration, the antitheses, and the poly-syllabic emphasis of 'sagacious', 'turbulent', and 'implac-able', all unite to give the words an air of authority, and even of finality, that overwhelms any possible objection. The cumulative effect of a sequence of such couplets is, of course, still more devastating. For rhetorical purposes—for gene-rating excitement, compelling assent, concentrating meaning —there is (or, until it went out of fashion, there was) no measure comparable in effectiveness to the heroic couplet.

Finally, Dryden greatly deepened the significance of his poem by finding a biblical parallel for the contemporary situation. When we feel that 'it has all happened before', the present event assumes an increased importance, and even a sort of inevitability that makes it appear more significant, and, as Dryden must have wished, more dangerous. 'Poesy', we are told by Bacon, '...is nothing else but feigned history.'[3] By basing his *Absalom and Achitophel* on true history, and applying actual events of the past to his own times, Dryden served his purpose far more effectively than he could have done if he had invented a fiction of his own. A story, too, that was taken from the Bible had a special sort of prestige—more especially, of course, for a generation that knew its Bible far better than most of us know ours today, and for whom the Old Testament was still a sacred book,

3

and not just an interesting collection of Hebrew literature. This last point is of some importance, for the biblical parallel gave still greater audacity to the daring wit of the poet who could compare Charles II with King David on the ground that both of them had fathered so many bastards. King David, we are told,

> His vigorous warmth did, variously, impart
> To Wives and Slaves; and, wide as his Command,
> Scatter'd his Maker's Image through the Land.[1]

And so, too, in his own amiable and undiscriminating fashion, had Charles II. All through the poem, indeed, the contemporary reader had the satisfaction of following Dryden's ingenious application of ancient history to current events and characters: a satisfaction similar to that which the readers of Pope's imitations of Horace or Johnson's imitations of Juvenal obtained from their substitution of modern names for those of ancient Rome.

In his two political satires Dryden, the Poet Laureate, served the King and his ministers. In *MacFlecknoe* (1678) he had written something for himself. This famous poem might be better described as a highly developed lampoon than a satire, and it may serve to remind us again how damaging and unjust a lampoon may be. Thomas Shadwell was certainly no poet, and he was no doubt a fat and lumbering toper. But if I had to name the twelve best English comic dramatists I think Shadwell would just creep in at the bottom of the list. Yet as soon as I say that, I realise that hardly anyone will believe me; it is too late—it has been too late since *MacFlecknoe* was published in 1682. But if *MacFlecknoe* is a lampoon, it is redeemed (whatever poor Shadwell may have thought) by its humour. Indeed, if

Shadwell had been a purely imaginary character we should have looked upon him as a great comic creation, for the Shadwell of *MacFlecknoe* really is, as has recently been suggested, 'a creature of the comic imagination'.[1] It is usual to think of wit as the satirist's most deadly weapon, and there is quite a lot of wit in this poem; but it may be questioned whether the sort of humour that oils Dryden's couplets in *MacFlecknoe* is not more effective. Wit may flash out from a man who has been hurt, but we are conscious, while he is giving pain, that he has been pained himself. What is so insulting in Dryden's treatment of Shadwell is his enormous good humour, his serene contemplation of this comic butt, his amused detachment, his almost unconscious superiority. Dryden tells us, somewhat surprisingly, in his 'Discourse concerning the Original and Progress of Satire' that he was 'naturally vindicative'.[2] We can easily suppose that he was annoyed with Shadwell (the two men had been bickering in print for some years);[3] but we cannot read *MacFlecknoe* without feeling that Shadwell is almost an excuse for the poem, and that what Pope said with a good deal less justification of the *Dunciad*, 'The poem was not made for these authors, but these authors for the poem',[4] is true of Dryden's mock-heroic fantasy.

In choosing to satirise Shadwell by representing him as the successor to Flecknoe on the throne of Dullness, Dryden was writing the first great mock-heroic poem in English. Shadwell is raised to an unsought dignity that he cannot sustain. It is a make-believe dignity, of course; the throne is the throne of dullness. But so subtly does Dryden go to work in the heroic idiom that the words constantly give us a confused impression of grandeur, and it is only after a

3-2

moment's reflection that we realise that what seemed to be praise is in fact denigration of the deadliest kind. The effect on the reader is one of a delighted, but slightly blurred, realisation that Shadwell is being quietly taken to pieces. Dryden works here by a comic transformation of values. Flecknoe's opening speech rests upon a sort of ironical 'Evil, be thou my good':

> Shadwell alone my perfect image bears,
> Mature in dullness from his tender years;
> Shadwell alone of all my Sons is he
> Who stands confirm'd in full stupidity.
> The rest to some faint meaning make pretence,
> But Shadwell never deviates into sense.
> Some Beams of Wit on other souls may fall,
> Strike through and make a lucid intervall;
> But Shadwell's genuine night admits no ray,
> His rising Fogs prevail upon the Day.[1]

This has some of the qualities most characteristic of heroic utterance, notably the absence of all qualifications, the firm insistence on the superlative and the unlimited. It is of the same order as Milton's description of the faithful Abdiel,

> Among innumerable false unmoved,
> Unshaken, unseduced, unterrified.

All the time the heroic verse of *MacFlecknoe* maintains the dignity of the utterance, making it difficult for us to realise immediately just what is being implied, and yet, when we realise the irony, magnifying its effect. The words themselves constantly create the comic ambivalence on which the whole of the passage just quoted depends. 'Perfect', 'mature', 'confirmed', 'genuine' and so on are all terms which we readily associate with positive virtue, and which therefore predispose our minds to admiration, or at least approval. But the perfect image turns out to be an image of the wretched Flecknoe, and Shadwell's maturity is the maturity of dullness, and what he is confirmed in is his stupidity, and what is genuine is the night, the darkness, in Shadwell's brain. Again Shadwell never deviates, he holds resolutely on, he does not swerve aside from the path. The word 'deviates' had already acquired something of the meaning that it now has in our hideous modern term 'deviationist'. Once more we are invited to form a favourable judgment, until we suddenly find that Shadwell never deviates—not into nonsense, but into sense. Sometimes Dryden reverses the process, and follows a word of direct denigration with a grandiose simile that again has the effect of concealing the snake in the grass:

> Besides, his goodly Fabrick fills the eye
> And seems design'd for thoughtless Majesty:
> Thoughtless as Monarch Oakes that shade the plain,
> And, spread in solemn state, supinely reign.[1]

Those monarch oaks come near to sheltering Shadwell from our ridicule; their spreading branches fill the mind with pleasurable contemplation, and for the moment, but only for the moment, we cannot see the satirical wood for the trees.

It would hardly be true to say that Dryden became a satirist owing to the turn of events; but though there are plenty of satirical strokes in his prologues and epilogues, and even in *The Hind and the Panther*, his sustained satire is concentrated mainly on Shadwell, Shaftesbury, and the other enemies of the King and the Duke of York, and all of that satire was crowded into a few remarkable years. It is a very different story with Pope, whose satire is spread over thirty years.

Although Pope came before the public innocently enough with his *Pastorals* of 1709, the satirist was beginning to show, if not his teeth, at any rate his claws, in the *Essay on Criticism*, published two years later. In *The Rape of the Lock*, three years after that, the claws are scarcely visible, but we have the fascinating and dangerous play of a quite remarkable kitten. Just about this time, too, he wrote his two imitations of the satires of Donne, though they were not published until many years later, and then, no doubt, in a much revised form. It was, however, in middle age that Pope wrote most of his satire. We may take the *Dunciad* of 1728 as conveniently marking the watershed between the poet of the delighted fancy and the moralist and satirist; it is the last work of Pope's which bears unmistakable signs of the young poet. It appeared just three days before his fortieth birthday, and he had been actively engaged in writing it for about eighteen months.

It was in *The Rape of the Lock*, at all events, that Pope's satirical wit first dazzled his contemporaries. When, in the course of time, Joseph Warton led the reaction against Pope in the second half of the eighteenth century it was this mock-epic poem that seemed to him to be Pope's most imaginative work. 'It is in this composition', he thought, 'Pope principally appears a Poet; in which he has displayed more imagination than in all his other works taken together.'[1] It is certainly something to get Warton to admit that a satirical poem can be imaginative, for it was part of his case against Pope that 'wit and satire are transitory and perishable, but nature and passion are eternal'.[2] But in fact the neo-classical poets are often at their most imaginative when they are writing satire, and more especially mock-heroic poems. The mock-heroic, like almost every other form of poetical utterance in the eighteenth century, had developed into a literary kind; but it was always a kind that allowed the poet plenty of freedom. He could take risks and revel in absurdities; he could, and he did, let the fancy roam.

In *The Rape of the Lock* Pope establishes, and maintains with wonderful steadiness, a world in which all the values are transposed. He assumes ironically the point of view of Belinda, a young lady of fashion, the same sort of young lady as the Belinda or Araminta of Congreve's first comedy, and we are at once in a world of fantasy where trifles become matters of the utmost moment, and where there is tragedy in a sick lapdog or a laddered stocking. Some dire disaster threatens Belinda, Ariel tells his fellow sylphs, but he is not yet sure what form it will take:

> Some dire Disaster, or by Force, or Slight,
> But what, or where, the Fates have wrapt in Night.
> Whether the Nymph shall break Diana's law,
> Or some frail China Jar receive a Flaw,
> Or stain her Honour, or her new Brocade,
> Forget her Pray'rs, or miss a Masquerade,
> Or lose her Heart, or Necklace, at a Ball;
> Or whether Heav'n has doom'd that Shock must fall.[1]

We get this delicious jumbling of values again in 'Puffs, Powders, Patches, Bibles, Billet-doux',[2] and indeed it recurs all through the poem, and is directly relevant to Pope's satirical purpose.

The Rape of the Lock, again, is sustained by the same order of fantasy as went to the making of *Gulliver's Travels*. When

Ariel enumerates the punishments reserved for careless sylphs we might be in Lilliput:

> Whatever Spirit, careless of his Charge,
> His Post neglects, or leaves the Fair at large,
> Shall feel sharp Vengeance soon o'ertake his Sins,
> Be stopt in Vials, or transfixt with Pins;
> Or plung'd in Lakes of bitter Washes lie,
> Or wedg'd whole Ages in a Bodkin's eye:
> Gums and Pomatums shall his Flight restrain,
> While clog'd he beats his silken Wings in vain....
> Or as Ixion fix'd, the Wretch shall feel
> The giddy Motion of the whirling Mill,
> In Fumes of burning Chocolate shall glow,
> And tremble at the Sea that froaths below.[1]

Here again the integrity of Pope's vision is unassailable; he has created a world with its own laws, its own mode of operation; a world that has been gently touched with what Coleridge called 'the sudden charm which accidents of light and shade...diffuse over a known and familiar landscape'.[2] The landscape here is a fine lady's dressing room, and the paraphernalia of feminine vanity are seen in the queer distorting light of the poet's satire. As an American critic has recently suggested, 'The English Augustans were, at their best and most characteristic, laughing poets of a heightened unreality', or of 'an inverted, chaotic reality'.[3]

In the *Dunciad* we meet with a grotesque world that is again poised precariously, but safely, between the real and the unreal. The range from grave to gay is wider than in *The Rape of the Lock*, the tone is more diversified; but there is the same topsy-turvy seriousness, and at times a kind of high-spirited gravity reminiscent of Swift. The vision of negation and darkness with which the poem ends is perhaps the highest reach of Pope's imagination. Although in the *Dunciad* Pope is seriously engaged in keeping up the standards of literature by ruthlessly exposing the inept and the dull and the charlatan, the poem is in some ways an extended lampoon. A naughty boy of genius is writing on walls. In no other of his poems does Pope expect quite so much private knowledge from his readers. It is true that he provided an elaborate commentary which often enables us to understand an allusion that might otherwise have been unintelligible, but he still leaves much unsaid. Sometimes he offers us no help at all, since to be explicit might be dangerous. When, for example, he substituted Colley Cibber for Theobald in the *Dunciad* of 1743, he had to rewrite the passage in which Theobald had sacrificed his works to the Goddess of Dullness. It is now Cibber who is taking one last look at *his* works before he sets fire to them with one of his Birth-day odes:

> O born in sin, and forth in folly brought!
> Works damn'd, or to be damn'd! (your father's fault)
> Go, purify'd by flames ascend the sky,
> My better and more Christian progeny!
> Unstain'd, untouch'd, and yet in maiden sheets;
> While all your smutty sisters walk the streets.[1]

Pope helps us to an understanding of 'my better and more Christian progeny' by referring to a passage in Cibber's *Apology*, where, with characteristic jauntiness, Cibber has told his readers that his Muse and his spouse were equally prolific; that 'the one was seldom the mother of a child, but in the same year, the other made me the father of a play'. But why was his literary progeny 'more Christian'? Because, one must suppose, Pope is thinking of Cibber's eldest son, the notorious Theophilus, and his youngest daughter Charlotte, Mrs Charlotte Charke, who was no better than she should be. The surface meaning of the next couplet is that the books Cibber is offering up as a sacrifice are clean copies that have never been exposed for sale, as distinct from those that have been cried about the Town by dirty-thumbed hawkers. I wish I could think that was all; but in view of the word 'smutty' and the well-known irregularities of Mrs Charke I believe she is further glanced at in the phrase 'walk the streets'.

To take one other example of Pope's open and halfconcealed allusions, there is a memorable description of Orator Henley in the third book of the *Dunciad*. Henley was an eccentric clergyman who appears to have grown impatient with his lot, and who therefore sought to give himself a more rapid preferment than any that seemed likely to come to him in the natural course of events, by opening what he called an Oratory in Newport Market, Butcher's Row. There, as Pope says in a long note, he 'preached on the Sundays theological matters and on the Wednesdays upon all other sciences'. Pope pictures him in his pulpit:

> Imbrown'd with native bronze, lo! Henley stands,
> Tuning his voice, and balancing his hands.[1]

'Native bronze' refers to Henley's dark complexion, and also implies his brazen-faced impudence. The second line describes the mountebank's action in the pulpit (he taught oratory), the word 'balancing' being at once precise (Pope is almost certainly describing what he had actually seen) and at the same time comically suggestive of a too deliberate artifice. The description proceeds mercilessly until Pope remembers Butcher's Row, and seizes upon it gratefully for yet another deadly thrust:

> But Fate with butchers plac'd thy priestly stall,
> Meek modern faith to murder, hack, and mawl.[1]

'Stall' suggests a booth or covered stand in an open street, with a huckster bawling out his joints and giblets to the passer-by. Henley's Oratory was a booth for the sale of shoddy religious provisions. But the second line carries with it a further suggestion which is not, perhaps, so obvious. 'Meek modern faith to murder, hack, and mawl': the butcher slaughtered cattle, cut up carcasses, and trimmed his joints and his chops with a cleaver. The word 'meek', however, suggests that the particular animal the poet has in mind here is the lamb, and I am afraid that Pope, who never willingly turned down a witty blasphemy, was thinking in this religious context of the *Agnus Dei*, the Lamb of God, suffering again at the hands of the unspeakable Henley.

In discussing only his two mock-heroic poems, I have of course got Pope rather out of focus. The greater part of his satirical work was written in the loose, discursive style that he had learnt from Horace. Long before Pope's day it had become a critical common-place to distinguish tragic satire (as written by Juvenal) from comic satire (as written by Horace). There is perhaps more of Juvenal in Pope's later work than is generally supposed; but after 1730 Horace became more and more his master, and Pope sometimes came as near to him as any English poet writing in the heroic couplet could hope to come. His preference for Horace was based on the Roman poet's studied ease, and the perfect good breeding of his diction. Horace was polite, a wit, a man of the world—pretty nearly everything that Pope wanted to be, and to a large extent succeeded in being. Horace, he had noticed in one of his own earliest poems,

> charms with graceful negligence,
> And without method talks us into sense.[1]

Pope himself often adopted the 'without method' method, but in the *Moral Essays* he chose to develop a particular theme. What is constant is the easy, conversational tone, a tone that almost paradoxically achieves the casual without for one moment relaxing the tension. To realise the sharpness and the delicacy of Pope's satire, and the variety and liveliness of his rhythm and his imagery, it is only necessary to compare him with one of the many other eighteenth-century writers of verse satire, such as Paul Whitehead, or even Edward Young. When we read Young's *Love of Fame the Universal Passion*, we may find ourselves wondering why we don't think better of it. Young is astute and sensible, he has telling things to say on every page; and yet he soon grows monotonous, and we become aware that our attention is beginning to wander. Formal verse satire, unsupported as it is by any narrative interest and therefore resting entirely on its own merits, must be of the finest quality if it is to be worth reading. Some friends of Pope are impatient because criticism has concentrated so exclusively on his style. They are right to protest if it is suggested that Pope has nothing to say; but they are wrong if they believe that Pope's thought would interest us much today if he had not laboured at his art more meticulously than perhaps any other English poet. As we must now take leave of him, let us leave him with some of his couplets ringing in our ears. I choose, as I must choose something, the lines that he wrote on those ladies of fashion who have now grown old, but who cannot, or will not, give up:

> At last, to follies Youth could scarce defend,
> It grows their Age's prudence to pretend;
> Asham'd to own they gave delight before,
> Reduc'd to feign it, when they give no more:
> As Hags hold Sabbaths, less for joy than spight,
> So these their merry, miserable Night;
> Still round and round the Ghosts of Beauty glide,
> And haunt the places where their Honour dy'd.[1]

There is no other voice quite like that in the whole of English poetry; no other poet with that merciless and controlled rhythm, that wicked wit, that nice discrimination, and that haunting suggestion of loveliness which softens the asperities of the moralist.

If there was no one to challenge Pope on his own chosen ground, there was still room for a professed imitator of Juvenal. In 1738 Samuel Johnson, a young bookseller's hack of twenty-eight years, published his *London*, and the poem sufficiently impressed Pope to make him enquire after the author, and try to give him some assistance. Five years after Pope's death appeared one of the great poems of the eighteenth century, Johnson's *Vanity of Human Wishes*. Into this sombre and powerful imitation of Juvenal's tenth satire Johnson poured his own experience of life and his own sad stoicism. Of this poem we might say what Johnson himself said of Dryden's poetry, that it is the result of 'a vigorous genius operating upon large materials'. Johnson's satire has great power and great control; it is charged with strong feeling, and its argument moves forward with a disciplined eloquence. The couplets clang like gongs, but everything is pondered, everything is relevant. To see how good *The Vanity of Human Wishes* is one has only to turn to Charles Churchill, a rapid and vigorous writer of the Juvenalian school, but with so little seriousness or weight of thought that the sense often seems to be only an echo of the sound.

A good deal of Churchill's satire is political, and in consequence highly personal. The political satirist is always tempted to take things too easily, for he has a public that is prepared to come at least half-way to meet him. He is playing upon passions that are already aroused, and if he hits the target at all he is sure of vociferous approval. The eighteenth century produced a great quantity of political satire in verse, and some of it is still readable. Early in the century an unknown author wrote one of the most delightful satirical poems in the language, 'The Vicar of Bray'; a poem that develops a satirical momentum with each successive stanza, and yet succeeds in maintaining an air of good-humoured contempt from beginning to end. Not much satire of the period has the control and economy and the admirable tone of 'The Vicar of Bray'; yet the discipline of verse composition enabled writers such as James Bramston, Paul Whitehead, Sir Charles Hanbury Williams, the authors of *Probationary Odes*, and John Wolcot ('Peter Pindar') to compose satirical poems which often reached a considerable degree of intensity in isolated couplets or stanzas, and occasionally in extended passages. Others, such as T. J. Mathias, whose *Pursuits of Literature* ran through numerous editions, owed their reputation almost entirely to their topical appeal, and perhaps as much to the vindictive notes appended to their verses as to the verses themselves, which were often, as George Steevens suggested, 'a peg to hang [the] notes upon'.[1]

So prolific a writer as Peter Pindar was bound to write much ephemeral satire, but with all his coarseness and rough facility he had a sense of humour that has preserved at least some of his work from decay. In *The Royal Tour* he has caught brilliantly the staccato utterance of George III, and something of his character. The King is pictured on the Esplanade at Weymouth:

> A sailor pops upon the Royal Pair,
> On crutches borne—an object of despair:
> His squalid beard, pale cheek, and haggard eye,
> Though silent, pour for help a piercing cry.

> 'Who, who are you? what, what? hae, what are you?'

> 'A man, my Liege, whom Kindness never knew.'

> 'A sailor! sailor, hae? you've lost your leg.'

> 'I know it, Sir—which forces me to beg.
> I've nine poor children, Sir, besides a wife—
> God bless them! the sole comforts of my life.'

> 'Wife and nine children, hae?—all, all alive?
> No, no, no wonder that you cannot thrive.
> Shame, shame, to fill your hut with such a train!
> Shame to get brats for others to maintain!
> Get, get a wooden leg, or one of cork:
> Wood's cheapest—yes, get wood, and go to work.
> But mind, mind Sailor—hae, hae, hae—hear, hear—
> Don't go to Windsor, mind, and cut one there:
> That's dangerous, dangerous—there I place my traps—
> Fine things, fine things, for legs of thieving chaps:
> Best traps, my traps—take care—they bite, they bite,
> And sometimes catch a dozen legs a night.'

> 'Oh! had I money, Sir, to buy a leg!'

> 'No money, hae? nor I—go beg—go beg.'

If George III was the dullest monarch who ever sat on the English throne, he can at least be said to have begotten more brilliant satire than any other English king. Peter Pindar's good-humoured contempt is as damaging as anything written about him up to the appearance of *The Vision of Judgment*.

By the middle of the eighteenth century satire had become a literary habit. In an age which had grown so accustomed to the voice of the satirist it was not surprising that some writers who had no special proclivity to satire should have taken to writing it, just as at the present day all sorts of clever young men who have very little interest in other people have taken to writing novels. It is, indeed, a problem of some nicety to decide how far the satirical element in some eighteenth-century poets, such as Gay, Chatterton, Cowper, and Crabbe, is natural to them, and how far it is the outcome of their literary environment. When we find John Gay—in his own fashion as 'frolic' and 'gentle' as Charles Lamb—denouncing the Parisian ladies in some desperate and determined couplets, we may suspect that what we are listening to is not Gay's natural voice at all:

> This next the spoils of fifty lovers wears,
> Rich Dandin's brilliant favours grace her ears;
> The necklace Florio's gen'rous flame bestow'd,
> Clitander's sparkling gems her fingers load;
> But now, her charms grown cheap by constant use,
> She sins for scarfs, clock'd stockings, knots, and shoes.
> This next, with sober gait and serious leer,
> Wearies her knees with morn and ev'ning prayer;
> She scorns th' ignoble love of feeble pages,
> But with three Abbots in one night engages....[1]

We must surely suppose that the author of *Rural Sports*, *The Shepherd's Week*, and *Trivia* is writing in this exaggerated way because he has deliberately assumed the indignation of the satirist, and is relying upon his memories of Juvenal rather than first-hand knowledge of the *beau monde* of Paris. Gay usually has himself much better in hand than this, and his normal attitude is one of amused detachment. The *nos haec novimus esse nihil* which he prefixed to *The Beggar's Opera* probably represents that attitude accurately enough. Gay was a born writer who took his *writing* seriously, but his ideas are important mainly for the fact that they gave him something to write about.

Cowper's case is rather different, for there was a good deal that Cowper wanted to say, and he was by no means unwilling to pass judgment on the world of his own day. When he is satirical, however, Cowper seems hardly to be in his proper element. It might not be true to say that the satirist must always be a man of the world; he must at least be capable of being shocked by what he sees and hears. But if he is shockable, he must also have a certain toughness of fibre, and a sense of proportion that will enable him to distinguish the serious fault from the trivial. Cowper has neither: he was easily hurt, and the basis from which he satirised his world was an intense and rather narrow evangelicalism. We should hardly expect good satire from, say, a member of the Lord's Day Observance Society; indeed, we might well be surprised to find any satire at all coming from such a quarter. When, therefore, Cowper launches a satirical attack on the man who wastes his time in playing chess,

> Trembling, as if eternity were hung
> In balance on his conduct of a pin;

or on those who
> pushing ivory balls
> Across a velvet level, feel a joy
> Akin to rapture, when the bauble finds
> Its destined goal of difficult access,[1]

we probably feel that his scorn is in excess of the occasion,
and that his intolerance indicates an unbalanced personality.
Again, when Cowper writes satirically of the scientists—

> Some drill and bore
> The solid earth, and from the strata there
> Extract a register, by which we learn
> That He who made it, and revealed its date
> To Moses, was mistaken in its age.
> Some, more acute and more industrious still,
> Contrive creation; travel Nature up
> To the sharp peak of her sublimest height,
> And tell us whence the stars; why some are fixed,
> And planetary some; what gave them first
> Rotation; from what fountain flowed their light.
> Great contest follows, and much learned dust
> Involves the combatants; each claiming Truth,
> And Truth disclaiming both; and thus they spend
> The little wick of life's poor shallow lamp,
> In playing tricks with Nature, giving laws
> To distant worlds, and trifling in their own.
> Is't not a pity now, that tickling rheums
> Should ever tease the lungs and blear the sight
> Of oracles like these?

—we are apt to feel that it is not the scientists who have lost
their sense of proportion, but the satirist. 'When I see such
games', the poet continues,

> Played by the creatures of a Power who swears
> That He will judge the earth, and call the fool
> To a sharp reckoning that has lived in vain;

And when I weigh this seeming wisdom well,
And prove it in the infallible result
So hollow and so false—I feel my heart
Dissolve in pity, and account the learn'd,
If this be learning, most of all deceived.[1]

The scientist 'has lived in vain'. What, then, should he have been doing? He should presumably have been meditating on God and the life to come, saving his immortal soul. What worried Cowper about the scientists was their tendency to weaken the authority of religion by referring everything to natural causes. Cowper's fears are understandable, but his attack on science is surely unreasonable. Not all scientists (Cowper himself cites Newton) had lost their faith in religion; and even if the danger existed, the abandonment of all scientific enquiry hardly seems the best solution. And even if it were the best, or the only, solution, satire would not appear to be the most effective way of enforcing it. Something more massive, at least, than the tart and agitated comments of Cowper is required.

The satirist normally takes his stand on some middle ground between two undesirable extremes; and he has to convince us not only that his victims are wrong, but that he himself is right. Effective satire has been written by a satirist who believes that everyone is out of step but himself, but if that is to be his attitude he must be a much more confident and self-reliant person than Cowper ever was, and he must be able to surprise us into accepting his unfamiliar and unpopular ideas by every kind of concealment and indirection. Cowper has little subtlety of approach. What we get from him, in fact, is rarely pure satire, but a mixture of satire and preaching which amounts to a sort of timid invective. 'Positiveness is a good quality for preachers and orators,' Swift asserted, 'because he that will obtrude his thoughts and reasons upon a multitude will convince others the more as he appears convinced himself';[1] but though Cowper is moved by sincere convictions his voice is not strong enough to convince others. In any case, satire and preaching go ill together: if the preacher is most effective when he shows strong feeling, the satirist is most devastating when he appears to be most completely disengaged. Cowper's curious blend of contempt and concern, of scorn and pity, may be seen again in some of his strictures on high society. After rebuking extravagance in dress, he proceeds to develop his attack on the gay world:

> There they are happiest who dissemble best
> Their weariness; and they the most polite
> Who squander time and treasure with a smile,
> Though at their own destruction. She that asks
> Her dear five hundred friends, contemns them all
> And hates their coming. They (what can they less?)
> Make just reprisals, and with cringe and shrug,
> And bow obsequious, hide their hate of her.
> All catch the frenzy, downward from her Grace,
> Whose flambeaux flash against the morning skies,
> And gild our chamber ceilings as they pass,
> To her who, frugal only that her thrift
> May feed excesses she can ill afford,
> Is hackneyed home unlackeyed; who in haste
> Alighting, turns the key in her own door,
> And, at the watchman's lantern borrowing light,
> Finds a cold bed her only comfort left.
> Wives beggar husbands, husbands starve their wives,
> On Fortune's velvet altar offering up
> Their last poor pittance—Fortune most severe

Of goddesses yet known, and costlier far
Than all that held their routs in Juno's Heaven!
So fare we in this prison-house, the world;
And 'tis a fearful spectacle to see
So many maniacs dancing in their chains.[1]

The effect of this passage is curiously mixed: the poet
appears to waver between condemnation and pity, between
a satirical detachment and the concern proper to a Christian
contemplating the profitless and soul-destroying ambitions
of the worldly. The facts on which his satire plays are real
enough; the light from the torches of the great lady's retinue
shining on the bedroom ceiling in the small hours looks like
a memory from his London boyhood, and the picture of the
other lady undressing in the dark has the sort of ruthless
persistence in driving a point home that we associate with
Pope. But the *general* tone of the passage is rather different:
Cowper has realised the 'weariness' of those fashionable
folk, and is shocked and distressed at the way they 'squander
time' at the risk of 'their own destruction'; their mode of
life is a sort of 'frenzy' in which a cold bed is the 'only
comfort left', and the whole mad misguided business is 'a
fearful spectacle!' It is surely in such anxious reflections
that we hear the true voice of Cowper. The satire is incidental, and we may suspect that there would be even less of
it if Cowper were not an eighteenth-century poet, and if
satire had not been the dominant literary mode.

With Crabbe it is sometimes difficult to decide whether he
is being satirical, or whether he is not just enjoying what
most people would consider ugly and repellent. Crabbe
takes a robust pleasure in facing facts, and though he is not
always content to record, but sometimes wishes to expose,

he is best described as a realist. In his early work, however, the tone is often satirical. *The Village*, after all, is intended to describe rural life 'as Truth will paint it, and as Bards will not', and the comment is frequently sharpened by the poet's conscious disagreement with Goldsmith and the other eighteenth-century poets who had idealised village life. But again, as with Gay and Cowper, the satirical note in Crabbe's work seems, as often as not, to have been caught from the age itself. So persistent was the satirical habit of mind in the eighteenth century that, when I come upon a passage in *The Village* in which Crabbe describes the East Anglian landscape, where 'the thin harvest waves its wither'd ears', and the rank weeds 'rob the blighted rye', and the nodding poppies 'mock the hope of toil', I can almost persuade myself that wanting anything better to satirise the poet has taken to satirising Nature. The heroic couplet, with its pronounced balance and antithesis, had been used so often for satirical purposes that it was now perhaps hardly possible to use it in any other way.

By Crabbe's day, the heroic couplet was, so to say, on its last feet. It was part of the secret of Byron's success that he found a new form and a new measure for English satire.

> I've often wish'd that I could write a book,
>   Such as all English people might peruse;
> I never should regret the pains it took,
>   That's just the sort of fame that I should choose:
> To sail about the world like Captain Cook,
>   I'd sling a cot up for my favourite Muse,
> And we'd take verses out to Demarara,
> To New South Wales, and up to Niagara.
>
> Poets consume exciseable commodities,
>   They raise the nation's spirit when victorious,

They drive an export trade in whims and oddities,
   Making our commerce and revenue glorious;
As an industrious and painstaking body 'tis
   That Poets should be reckon'd meritorious:
And therefore I submissively propose
To erect one Board for Verse and one for Prose.

That, I hope we may agree, is the Byronic note; the new rhythm, and the colloquial, off-hand manner that proved so attractive to the readers of the early nineteenth century. But of course it is not Byron at all. The lines just quoted are the two opening stanzas of Hookham Frere's *Whistlecraft*, which had appeared in 1817, and which, as Byron himself acknowledged, first turned his mind to the suitability of *ottava rima* for satirical purposes. No doubt he had also met with the stanza in the Italian burlesque and satirical poets from Pulci to Casti. But what is of much more importance is that Byron's discovery of *ottava rima* obviously enabled him to bring much more of himself—one might almost say the whole of himself—into his poetry. It is true that he had always paraded some sort of self before the public, but in *Don Juan* it came much nearer to being 'the real Lord Byron'. It is significant that when Lady Blessington met him for the first time in 1823 she was disappointed. She had a vision of her own, and Byron had undone it. On reflection, however, she realised that if the man she had just met was difficult to reconcile with the poet of *Childe Harold* and *Manfred*, she could very easily imagine him as the author of *Beppo* and *Don Juan*. 'He is witty, sarcastic, and lively enough for these works, but he does not look like my preconceived notion of the melancholy poet.'[1] Several of his friends and acquaintances were struck with the resemblance of *Don Juan* to his own brilliant conversation. Without the *ottava rima* we might never have had this witty, drawling, casually preposterous conversation of Byron's in print.

The colloquial rhythm, the happy-go-lucky double and triple rhymes, the easy effrontery, the erratic and spontaneous association of unexpected ideas, all give to his satirical writing that contemptuous, off-hand manner which is its special virtue. This was something very nearly new in English satire, and wonderfully effective. The danger of tragical satire is that it gives the victim too much importance; and to feel important is a considerable consolation, and even a form of protection. We can put up with denunciation, for then we are at least being taken seriously; but to be dismissed as a sort of dull joke is highly insulting. I have suggested that Byron's off-hand, contemptuous manner was the new note in English satire. We met with something not unlike it in *MacFlecknoe*, and we shall meet with something still closer to Byron's cool effrontery and patrician indifference in some of the writers of Restoration comedy. The saying of outrageous things in a casual, unemphatic fashion is a habit most commonly found in the aristocrat.

Byron was in an ideal position for satirising English life; he had a long experience of it, and he had got away from it. The Frenchman or the American can satirise the English, and he does; but the most penetrating satire of national habits or national character often comes from an intelligent renegade. The expatriate can see more clearly than the foreigner the good and the bad in what he has left behind him; if he has unpleasant memories of the country of his origin, he is now detached from it, and if his satire comes from an over-flow of painful emotions recollected in Italy, what was once painful will have become pleasurable. Every satirist to some extent separates himself spiritually from the community in which he lives; but when, like Byron, he has separated himself physically from the land of his birth, while still retaining a vivid recollection of the natives, he has all the advantages, and none of the disadvantages, of the ivory tower. Byron's finest work, to my mind, is *The Vision of Judgment*. But his ultimate limitation as a satirist is that the only thing that interested him profoundly was himself.

Byron is the last great name in English verse satire. In a more congenial atmosphere than that of the Victorian age A. H. Clough might have written more of the original and polished satire that we get in his *Dipsychus*. Thomas Hardy, too, had a satirical streak that appears variously in *The Dynasts* and in many of his short poems, but also in such odd books as *The Hand of Ethelberta*.* But Hardy was always passing beyond the sharply focused vision of satire to a sardonic contemplation or to an Olympian pity for mankind in its desperate struggle with the nature of things. In more recent times the voice of the satirist has been heard again in such writers as Siegfried Sassoon and Roy Campbell, and still more recently in W. H. Auden; but most frequently, perhaps, the modern poet stops short of satire in a sort of no-man's-land of the ironical, leaving one with the feeling that he is 'willing to wound, and yet afraid to strike'. It may well be that the modern poet is too

---

* From what little we know of it, Hardy's first unpublished novel was a very surprising thing, much more like an early novel of Bernard Shaw's than the sort of story we usually associate with him.

tentative and exploratory, too unsure of his own beliefs, to commit himself to satire. The satirist, at least, must know his own mind, and know it before he begins to write. Whatever may be true of some kinds of poetry, no poet is likely to write a good satirical poem if he only knows what he wanted to say when the last word of the poem is written.

IV

PROSE SATIRE

Prose satire in England was slow to develop. There is nothing in the sixteenth century except More's *Utopia* to set beside such works of European reputation as the *Epistolae Obscurorum Virorum*, *The Praise of Folly*, or the *Gargantua and Pantagruel* of Rabelais. The *Utopia* is in part a straightforward protest against what the late Professor Chambers called 'the new statesmanship'[1] of early sixteenth-century Europe, and in part a complaint about the social and economic condition of England at the close of the Middle Ages. Where it is satirical, the satire has often been understood too literally, for More is one of those satirists who has sometimes been too clever for his readers. In general, he invites us to admire his Utopians, but occasionally he is simply making use of them to bring home to his sixteenth-century readers the hideousness of European civilisation. In the section in which he deals with the Utopian attitude to war he expects us to use our intelligence, and not to assume that the Utopians are invariably to be admired. He begins by telling us that they account war a beastly thing, and utterly despise military glory. So far, so good. But then we learn that they are never so proud as when they 'vanquishe and oppresse their enemies by craft and deceite'. Then, indeed, they *do* boast; for if they had nothing better than their bodily strength to brag about they would be no better than lions, boars, wolves, dogs, and other wild beasts. Accordingly, they always try to bribe and corrupt their enemies, and they scatter proclamations in enemy territory promising great rewards to anyone who will assassinate his prince. Does More approve of all this? Surely he is not asking us to take the Utopians as a pattern here, but to realise the full beastliness of war. So long as war is regarded as being glorious and chivalrous, so long will it continue; the Utopians, being a reasonable people, go to war with the utmost reluctance, but once involved, they have no romantic ideas about it. The writer of Utopian satire has usually felt himself free to use his imaginary inhabitants as patterns of virtue or as the exact opposite; he can make his points either way, as Swift was to do in *Gulliver's Travels*, and Samuel Butler in *Erewhon*. If More has been less well understood than most satirists, it may be because he adds a further complication of his own by frequently putting up ideas to be shot at, without committing himself in any way. He was a merry man, a joker, what is called a 'character', and in the *Utopia* he is sometimes no more than half serious.

The next hundred years have little to offer us. I have already made a few comments on Elizabethan prose satire,* but I ought to mention Thomas Dekker, whose satirical observation of London characters and manners in *The Seven Deadly Sins of London* and *The Gull's Hornbook* suggests that two centuries later he might have been a novelist of distinction. That traditional theme, the satire of women, is delightfully represented in the Elizabethan period by *The Batchelars Banquet*; but as this is a fairly close translation of a late medieval work, *Les Quinze Joyes de Mariage*, it can hardly be discussed here.[1]

Dekker's satirical pieces, with their acute character

* See pp. 33 ff.

sketches of London types, should remind us that among the favourite literary genres of the seventeenth century was the prose character, and that those characters, when written by such men as Sir Thomas Overbury, Earle, and above all Samuel Butler, were often salted with a considerable mixture of satirical wit. That they have lasted so well is due both to the wit and the observation; and their brevity, too, encouraged good writing, although it occasionally led to mannerism and over-writing. So far as satire is concerned, the character-writer's sustained attempt at discrimination and definition must have led to a considerable refinement in the satirical treatment of human character.

In the later seventeenth century, satirical prose becomes more common. Much of it, admittedly, is more a matter of banter and repartee than true satire; and here I would include Marvell's long and tedious reply to Bishop Parker, *The Rehearsal Transprosed*. To answer an opponent point by point, as Marvell does here, to quote his own words at length and then try to turn them against him with a quip that would require careful annotation to make it intelligible to the modern reader, is to invite the neglect of posterity. Marvell, of course, was not writing for posterity in *The Rehearsal Transprosed* (few satirists ever are); but even by the standards of political and ecclesiastical controversy it is something of a hybrid. You can either ridicule your opponent, in which case you can afford to be brief, or you can take him seriously, in which case you will have to answer his arguments fully. What you cannot do is to mix argument with ridicule at such length as Marvell does, without destroying the seriousness of the argument and losing the effect of the ridicule. *The Rehearsal Transprosed* is to Marvell's work what *The Parson's Tale* is to Chaucer's; it is there, it cannot be altogether ignored, but it is now little more than a literary curiosity. If, on the other hand, it was Marvell who wrote *His Majesty's Most Gracious Speech to Both Houses of Parliament* (1675), he wrote one of the cleverest political squibs of the period. This short piece is a parody of one of Charles II's addresses from the throne, and is, inevitably, concerned with his financial troubles. He has spent all that parliament voted him on the previous occasion:

Here's my Lord Treasurer can tell that all the Money design'd for next Summer's Guards must of Necessity be apply'd to the next Year's Cradles and Swaddling-Cloaths. What shall we do for Ships then? I hint this only to you, it being your Business, not mine. I know by Experience I can live without Ships; I liv'd Ten Years abroad without, and never had my Health better in my Life. But how *you* will be without I leave to your selves to judge, and therefore hint this only by the by; I don't insist upon it.[1]

There are numerous other short pieces, such as *The Humble Address of the Atheists* (1688, successfully exposing James II's Declaration of Indulgence), which show considerable wit, and also serve to indicate that there was by now a public ready to appreciate this sort of ingenious commentary on current events. Among those minor prose satires, one of the subtlest is *The Memoirs of Monsieur Duval*, by the facetious Dr Walter Pope. Duval, a highwayman, who was turned off at Tyburn in 1670, had won the hearts of the Restoration ladies, and it is against them that Walter Pope's satire is directed. It is not known whether Fielding had read it, but, if he had, its ironical commendation of Duval may have given him some hints for his own *Jonathan Wild*.

And so we arrive at the age of Defoe and Swift, of

Addison and Steele, the great age of satirical journalism in periodicals and pamphlets. Defoe came from a class that rarely meddles with satire at all; he was of middle-class trading stock, and the son of a Presbyterian. In 1701 he had scored a remarkable popular success with *The True-born Englishman*, a long verse satire in which he replied to those who objected to King William's Dutch favourites and were crying 'England for the English', by reminding them that the English were a mongrel race in any event, a mixture of Saxons, Danes, Normans, Scots, Picts, and what not. In 1702 he ventured into more dangerous waters. With the accession of Queen Anne, the Dissenters, who had achieved a measure of toleration under William of Orange, found themselves facing a new crisis. During the reign of William and Mary they had been allowed to qualify for military and civil offices by practising what was called occasional conformity. This typically English compromise required the Dissenter only to take Communion occasionally within the Church of England, and left him free for the rest of the year to worship in his own meeting-house. But now, with a new Queen on the throne and the Tory party in the ascendant, a bill to prevent occasional conformity was introduced into the House of Commons, and the High Church divines began denouncing the Dissenters and calling for measures to suppress them altogether. It was at this stage, in December 1702, when feelings in the country were running high, that a pamphlet appeared with the uncompromising title, *The Shortest Way with the Dissenters*. The unknown author outdid even the High Church divines in the bitterness of his attack:

'Tis vain to trifle in this matter. The light foolish handling of them by mulcts, fines, etc., 'tis their glory and advantage. If the gallows instead of the Counter, and the gallies instead of fines were the reward of going to a conventicle, to preach or hear, there would not be so many sufferers. The spirit of martyrdom is over; they that will go to church to be chosen for sheriffs and mayors would go to forty churches rather than be hanged.

Not unnaturally, the High Church party were delighted with this anonymous supporter; but when, a few weeks later, it was discovered that the author was in fact one of the Dissenters, Daniel Defoe, and that the pamphlet was an ironical *reductio ad absurdum* of their own extravagant demands, they called for his punishment. What Defoe had done, in fact, was to satirise the High Church divines by a slightly exaggerated imitation of their habitual mode of thought and expression. He may be said to have faked a High Church pamphlet, and done it so successfully that it was accepted as genuine. When political or religious opinions have grown to be quite preposterous, the ordinary techniques of satire become ineffective, and some more drastic method is required to bring home to the extremist how outrageous those opinions really are. *The Shortest Way* came very near to achieving this end, and Defoe was made to suffer for it. He was found guilty of publishing a seditious libel, fined, sentenced to stand three times in the pillory, and given an indefinite term of imprisonment. So dangerous is irony, and so exasperating is it to most people to be the victims of a practical joke. But Defoe was unlucky. The Tories, to use an American expression, had been 'gunning for' him for some years, and his sentence was clearly a cumulative one for past offences. Ironically enough, the people most shocked were his fellow Dissenters, from whom he got almost no sympathy at all. The Protestant seems always to have been less willing than the Roman Catholic to have religious subjects treated in anything but a solemn fashion, and among Protestants the nonconformist is probably the least willing of all.

Defoe ought to have learnt his lesson; but not many years later he was in trouble again for an almost identical mistake. In 1713, when the question of who was to succeed Queen Anne was growing urgent, Defoe, a convinced upholder of the Hanoverian succession, published in rapid sequence three anonymous pamphlets. The title of the first was *Reasons against the Succession of the House of Hanover*, and of the second, *And What if the Pretender should Come? Or Some Consideration of the Advantages and Real Consequences of the Pretender's Possession of the Crown of Great Britain*. Both titles, and the second especially, remind one of Swift's *Argument to Prove that the Abolishing of Christianity may, as things now stand, be attended with some Inconveniences*, and both pamphlets were ironical throughout. This time it was the Whigs who were exasperated with him, and Defoe spent another brief spell in prison before he could convince the court that he had been writing satire.

Those satirical pieces are exceptions with Defoe; irony was not his habitual mode of expression, and when he did write ironically he made such an artistic success of it that he exposed himself to all the dangers of misunderstanding. With Swift we reach an author who almost habitually expressed himself in ironical statement.

In the Preface to *The Battle of the Books* Swift admits that 'Satyr is a sort of glass, wherein beholders do generally discover everybody's face but their own; which is the chief reason for that kind reception it meets with in the world,

4

and that so very few are offended with it.' It is obvious that
if the satirist is a man who wishes to mend the world he must
fail in his attempt if the more he cracks the whip the more
the spectators sit back and laugh. One of the satirist's main
problems, therefore, is how to touch the conscience of his
reader, how to make the reader apply the satire to himself.
The problem as I have just stated it is one that is chiefly
relevant to the writer of general satire, and it is to that category that most of Swift's satirical writings belong.[1] With particular or personal satire the question of its application does
not arise, or it takes a different form; the victim is named,
or is at least easily recognisable. The problem here will be
how to expose the person satirised so as to convince all
fair-minded readers that he is really contemptible, and is not
being attacked out of mere spite or for purely party reasons,
and also how to shame the victim into some sort of reformation, or at least to check him in his confident wickedness.

To see Swift's personal satire at its most lethal we cannot
do better than turn to his *Short Character of his Excellency
Thomas Earl of Wharton*. This able and unscrupulous politician was one of Swift's *bêtes-noires*, and yet Wharton seems
to have compelled some sort of unwilling admiration (though
certainly not respect) from Swift. The effectiveness of the
attack is due in part to the assumed carelessness with which
it is delivered; Swift is apparently *dégagé*, imperturbable,
and so he is able to give an impression of complete impartiality. 'His Excellency', he tells us

is one whom I neither personally love nor hate. I see him at
Court, at his own house, and sometimes at mine (for I have the
honour of his visits), and when these papers are public, it is odds
but he will tell me, as he did once upon a like occasion, that he is

damnably mauled; and then, with the easiest transition in the world, ask about the weather, or the time of the day: so that I enter on the work with more chearfulness because I am sure neither to make him angry, nor any way hurt his reputation; a pitch of happiness and security to which His Excellency hath arrived, and which no philosopher before him could reach.

The tone is scrupulously just—or, more accurately, it seems to be entirely judicial; but already there are gleams of irony playing on the surface. Swift says he is confident that he cannot hurt Wharton's reputation. What exactly, we find ourselves asking, does he mean by that? Already, too, we begin to be aware of what is to be Swift's chief method in dealing with this dissolute and shameless nobleman: he appears to praise him, and to some extent he is perhaps unconsciously acknowledging certain desirable qualities in Wharton's character. Wharton is easy and good-natured; he is not readily put out by criticism, or ruffled by attacks. One remembers a passage in the *Journal to Stella* where Swift remarked, with a sort of envy, on the imperturbability of Harley and St John in a period of acute political crisis. 'I cannot but think they have mighty difficulties upon them,' he confides to Stella, 'yet I always find them as easy and disengaged as schoolboys on a holiday.'[1] There, surely, we have the man of letters admiring the men of action, so different from his own worrying self. There may be something of this unwilling admiration in the *Character of Wharton*. What is not in doubt is the extent to which the condemnation of Wharton's character is achieved by what appears at first sight to tell in his favour, but what a moment later is seen to be an additional reason for despising the man. Swift allows us for a few moments to remain in doubt about

4-2

87

his real meaning, or even to misunderstand it, so that the next moment he can crash it home with direct and quite unambiguous denunciation.

Thomas Earl of Wharton, Lord Lieutenant of Ireland, by the force of a wonderful constitution, hath passed some years his grand climacterick without any visible effects of old age, either on his body or his mind, and in spite of a continual prostitution to those vices which usually wear out both. His behaviour is in all the forms of a young man at five and twenty. Whether he walketh, or whistleth, or sweareth, or talketh bawdy, or calleth names, he acquitteth himself in each beyond a Templar of three years standing. With the same grace, and in the same style, he will rattle his coachman in the middle of the street, where he is governor of the kingdom; and all this without consequence, because it is in his character, and what every body expecteth. He seemeth to be but an ill dissembler and an ill liar, although they are the two talents he most practiseth, and most valueth himself upon. The ends he hath gained by lying appear to be more owing to the frequency, than the art of them; his lies being sometimes detected in an hour, often in a day, and always in a week. He tells them freely in mixed companies, although he knows half of those that hear him to be his enemies, and is sure they will discover them the moment they leave him. He sweareth solemnly he loveth and will serve you; and your back is no sooner turned, but he tells those about him you are a dog and a rascal. He goeth constantly to prayers in the forms of his place, and will talk bawdy and blasphemy at the chapel door. He is a presbyterian in politicks, and an atheist in religion; but he chuseth at present to whore with a papist. . . .

There we can see the process at work. We all agree that it is a good thing a man should have a vigorous constitution, and Wharton has one. How do we know? Because if he hadn't a robust constitution he would have worn it out long ago by a lifetime of debauchery. It is a good thing that a man should

carry his years lightly: Wharton carries his so well that he
behaves at the age of sixty-three like an adolescent. We
admire a man who cannot dissemble or lie: we therefore
ought to admire Wharton because he has no talent for either.
It is queer, though, that he shouldn't be better at it, for he
spends all his time trying to deceive people. *The Character*
has never been subjected to much critical analysis, and
passing references to it as a 'ferocious attack' hardly suggest
that the subtlety of its technique has been fully appreciated.
Swift rarely gives us anything so crude as simple invective,
preferring with Horace some indirect form of ridicule. As
he wrote himself,

> Bastings heavy, dry, obtuse,
> Only Dulness can produce,
> While a little gentle Jerking
> Sets the Spirits all a working.[1]

It is unlikely that Swift's attack made a deep impression on
Wharton; but if he was able to laugh it off he was a remarkable man.

Another of Swift's most damaging exercises in personal
satire, though in quite a different vein, was his exposure of
Partridge the astrologer. Here he had taken a hint from
Tom Brown and some other wits who made fun of Partridge's
Predictions about a dozen years earlier; but it was Swift who
realised, in a moment of inspiration, that the way to finish
off Partridge was to pose as a rival astrologer and issue a
mock prediction of his death. This he proceeded to do in
Isaac Bickerstaff's Predictions for the Year 1708. 'My first
prediction is but a trifle,' Mr Bickerstaff wrote, 'yet I will
mention it to show how ignorant these sottish pretenders to
Astrology are in their own concerns. It relates to Partridge

the almanac-maker. I have consulted the stars of his nativity by his own rules, and I find he will infallibly die upon the 29th of March next, about eleven at night, of a raging fever.' Swift followed this up with an *Elegy on the Death of Partridge* which was selling in the streets of London on the morning of March 30th, and drove the point home further with a pamphlet called *The Vindication of the First of Mr Bicker-staff's Prophecies*. The joke was kept up for several months with still further pamphlets; and the whole episode must be the perfect example of hoisting a man with his own petard. One mark of the great satirist is that he sees the most effective way of getting through his opponent's guard, and another is that he seizes every casual opening to land his punches. In the Bickerstaff pamphlets Swift does both of those things to perfection. It was characteristic of him, too, to proceed by a sort of jujitsu method, by which the victim of his satire was thrown by his own weight. As for the effect of the Bickerstaff pamphlets, overwhelming ridicule was the only way to stop Partridge, and in fact Swift appears to have succeeded in putting him out of business. His name was struck off the Register at Stationers' Hall, and the Company took over the right of publishing his almanac. Partridge protested that he was still alive; but, as Swift pointed out, 'if an uninformed carcass walks still about, and is pleased to call it self Partridge, Mr Bickerstaff does not think himself any way answerable for that'. The stars, in fact, could not lie.

Although Swift was sometimes provoked into exposing the individual, his satire is more often general than personal. Of *A Tale of a Tub* I will only say that it has always seemed to me one of those books which it is more fun to write than to read. It is obviously characteristic of the Rabelaisian side of Swift, but it is not at all typical of his satire as a whole. Compared with the *Argument against Abolishing Christianity* or *Gulliver's Travels* or the *Modest Proposal*, where Swift holds to his theme with an undeviating sense of relevance, *A Tale of a Tub* is an undisciplined and self-indulgent work. It does, however, by its very waywardness and provocative individuality bring home to us the very personal nature of Swift's humour. He was always something of a puzzle to his contemporaries, and it is significant that one of the women who knew him best remarked that no human creature was capable of guessing his thoughts because 'never anyone living thought like him'.[1] Swift was unpredictable; and one of the main reasons for his unpredictability was his odd and individual sense of humour. 'People are scandaliz'd', he once observed, 'if one laughs at what they call a serious thing. Suppose I were to have my Head cut off tomorrow, and all the World were talking of it today, yet why might I not laugh to think, *What a bustle is here about my Head?*'[2] One can only say that if Swift could find such a situation amusing, very few other people would be likely to achieve such detachment in similar circumstances. Swift seems also to have had what was rather unusual in the eighteenth century, an almost complete disregard for conventional attitudes; and when he found how much the unconventional startled the conventionally minded he may have deliberately cultivated it still further. He appears to have been honestly surprised at the fuss made about the religious satire in the *Tale of a Tub*; it had not occurred to him that so many readers would be scandalised. Even Pope, who knew him better than most people, once remarked on his 'odd blunt way', and proceeded to illustrate it by. an anecdote which certainly suggests a deliberate eccentricity. 'One evening', Pope explained,

Gay and I went to see him: you know how intimately we all were acquainted. On our coming in, 'Hey-day, gentlemen,' says the Doctor, 'what's the meaning of this visit? How come you to leave all the great lords that you are so fond of, to come hither to see a poor Dean?'

'Because we would rather see you than any of them.'

'Ay, any one that did not know you as well as I do might believe you. But since you are come, I must get some supper for you, I suppose?'

'No, Doctor, we have supped already.'

'Supped already! that's impossible: why, 'tis not eight o'clock yet.'

'Indeed, we have.'

'That's very strange: but if you had not supped I must have got something for you. Let me see, what should I have had? a couple of lobsters? ay, that would have done very well—two shillings: tarts—a shilling. But you will drink a glass of wine with me, though you have supped so much before your usual time, only to spare my pocket?'

'No, we had rather talk with you than drink with you.'

'But if you had supped with me, as in all reason you ought to have done, you must have drank with me. A bottle of wine—two shillings. Two and two is four; and one is five: just two and sixpence apiece.—There, Pope, there's half-a-crown for you; and there's another for you, sir: for I won't save any thing by you I am determined.'

That was all said and done with his usual seriousness on such occasions; and in spite of everything we could say to the contrary, he actually obliged us to take the money.[1]

In a satirist, no doubt, eccentricity in a pronounced degree must be looked upon as some sort of limitation. Readers must not be left groping in the dark. Satire is difficult enough for many people as it is; it normally employs some form of indirect statement, and it can only work if the reader is able to penetrate behind the irony to the intention of the satirist.

No reader need have been in any doubt about *The Battle of the Books*, where the satire is both general and personal. This is a highly successful exercise in belittlement, at once gratifying the visual imagination, and effectively ridiculing a literary controversy. Swift's aim here is almost purely destructive; his intention is much more to maul Bentley and Wotton than to take sides with the Ancients against the Moderns. He does, it is true, pronounce upon the issue in the fable of the spider and the bee, but his essential purpose is to make the whole controversy appear trivial, a mere battle of books. Sir William Temple had been made to look foolish, and Swift decided that if he was to be defended the best form of defence here was attack. Similarly, when Pope's shortcomings as an editor of Shakespeare are exposed by Theobald a generation later, he does not argue the case on its merits, but writes the *Dunciad* to ridicule (among other things) pedantry and verbal criticism.

In general, Swift's satirical intentions are not in doubt, except on two important accounts. The first is that irony always baffles the dull and the stupid; and the second is that in most of his satires the writer or speaker is not Swift himself, but some *persona* that he has assumed for the occasion. If we do not realise who the *persona* is, and what he represents, we shall misunderstand the irony, and so, inevitably, misinterpret Swift's satirical intentions. Let us suppose that one day a pamphlet is published with the rather curious but arresting title, *An Argument to Prove that the Abolishing of the University of Cambridge may, as things now stand, be attended with some inconveniences, and perhaps not produce those many Good Effects proposed thereby.* If we came across that pamphlet in a Cambridge bookshop we should probably suspect that it was ironical. If we started to read it, and found that the first reason offered for preserving the University was that if it ceased to exist there would be no annual Boat Race, our suspicion that there was something ironical here might be confirmed. And if we were to read on and find the author answering the arguments of the abolitionists in words which might almost have been written by Swift himself—

It is likewise urged, that there are by computation, in this university, above a thousand dons, whose revenues would suffice to maintain at least two hundred young gentlemen of wit and pleasure....This indeed appears to be a consideration of some weight. But then, on the other side, several things deserve to be considered likewise: as, first, whether it may not be thought necessary that in certain tracts of country there should be some at least of abilities to read and write....And pray, what would become of the race of men in the next age if we had nothing to trust to besides the scrofulous and consumptive productions furnished by our men of wit and pleasure? Now here are one thousand persons reduced by taxation to a low diet and moderate exercise, who are the only great restorers of our breed, without which the nation would in an age or two become but one great hospital.

—if we had read as far as that, we should no longer be in any doubt that the author was writing ironically. Yet we might still be in some uncertainty about the exact standpoint from which he was writing. Is he, we might have to ask ourselves, a self-made man who objects to all universities as such? Or is he only an Oxford man who doesn't think much of

Cambridge? Or is he perhaps a Cambridge man who believes that his old university would be truer to its ancient traditions if it did less well in the Boat Race and better in the tripos lists? It is quite clear that in some way or other he is critical of Cambridge, but what is he *for?*

Questions of just that sort confront the reader of Swift's *Argument against the Abolishing of Christianity*, and Swift makes it more difficult for us to find the right answer by occasionally shifting his ground. In reading his satires we must never take up a rigid position, and we must never assume that Swift will do so either. The voice that we hear at the beginning of the *Argument against Abolishing Christianity* is clearly enough that of a man of the world who believes that a state religion makes for social and political stability, but who is careful to tell us that what he has undertaken to defend is not real, but nominal, Christianity. He hopes that no reader will think him weak enough to stand up in defence of real Christianity. 'To offer at the restoring of that, would indeed be a wild project; it would be to dig up foundations, to destroy at one blow all the wit and half the learning of the kingdom'—to ruin trade, to empty the law-courts and the stock exchange, and so on. As we read on, we realise that the position of the writer is that of the deists or free-thinkers, whom Swift abominated; but it has also been maintained convincingly that the *Argument* is directed against the Whigs who, in 1708, were contemplating the repeal of the Test Act—the act which made the holding of any military or civil office conditional upon receiving the sacrament of the Church of England. There is no need to decide between those alternatives; Swift probably had both in mind when he wrote his pamphlet. At all events, he frequently shifted his aim in his satires, and we have to be ready to adapt ourselves to the change of direction; he is like someone who goes out rook-shooting, but doesn't hesitate to bring down a pigeon if it happens to cross the line of fire. There is a further complication. Once or twice he appears to drop the pretence altogether, and the voice we hear is his own. When, for example, near the beginning of the pamphlet, the writer asks: 'Would any indifferent foreigner who should read the trumpery lately written by Asgill, Tindall, Toland, Coward, and forty more, imagine the Gospel to be our rule of faith?' he is not writing like a freethinker, for the 'trumpery' in question is the work of the deistical writers he has named. On this occasion Swift's lapse from make-believe was probably intentional; if he had said 'the *admirable* works of Asgill, Tindall, and so forth' he might have been taken literally. On some other occasions when the mask is suddenly dropped, he may simply have forgotten.

What especially distinguishes Swift's satire is his ability to insinuate his ideas into the mind of his reader, and this is largely a matter of finding the form that suits them best. I take two examples, one long and the other quite short: *Gulliver's Travels* and the *Modest Proposal*. In *Gulliver's Travels* Swift's chosen vehicle is, of course, the imaginary voyage. If you wish to offer your reader a comprehensive criticism of his own country, its manners, morals, and institutions, you cannot do better than land him in a strange country, where you can then proceed to contrast the natives with his own fellow-countrymen. You will have all the advantages both of resemblance and difference, the resemblance enabling you to make your points by dwelling on what is, *mutatis mutandis*, familiar, and the difference helping you to drive home the satirical contrast. But in *Gulliver's Travels* Swift made a more absolute break with the familiar than is customary; his traveller found himself among Lilliputians, giants, horses, and on a flying island, and the challenge to his art consisted in finding how to make the average, moderately imaginative reader accept the abnormal situation, and not reject it out of hand as merely ridiculous. Swift attains this end partly by adopting the method of gradualism. He lets us into the strange new environment step by step, authenticating it by careful attention to detail and measurements, and so fascinating us with the picturesque or grotesque fact that our imagination contributes to our deceit. It has all happened as inevitably and imperceptibly as a change in the weather. A good deal is due to the gravity of the narrator, and it is here that Lemuel Gulliver is so important. Swift realised that he must not make his traveller a fool or a figure of fun. Gulliver is a very fair representative of the English race, rather above than below the average in intelligence and experience. He was, to begin with, a Cambridge man; he had been up at Emmanuel College for three years, where, as he tells us, he had applied himself closely to his studies, and though he left without taking a degree we are not to hold that against him.[1] Gulliver, at any rate, had to be sensible and well informed if he was to converse adequately with the King of the Brobdingnagians and his Master among the Houyhnhnms. (I may remark in passing that Gulliver's way of referring to the horses is a beautiful example of what I have called Swift's gradualism. When Gulliver first catches sight of them in Chapter I they are just horses to him, and he tries to stroke one, 'using the common style and whistle of jockeys when they are going to handle a strange horse'. In Chapter II they are still nags and mares to him, though by this time he is considerably shaken; but before long he is conducted to what at first he calls 'the master horse', and then, by an easy but immensely significant transition, 'my master'. From now on it is always 'my master'; the normal relationship has been reversed so quietly that perhaps most readers have never noticed it happening.) If Gulliver had been an unfavourable specimen of humanity, stupid, ignorant, vulgar, or brutal, we should have had an alibi, and the satire would have lost much of its point. But although he necessarily has his limitations, imposed by the demands of the satire (he has to be shown as rather a naïve admirer of his own dear country, aware of all the damning evidence without drawing any of the obvious conclusions), his grave, steady ordinariness and decency contribute very considerably to the credibility of the four narratives.

In *A Modest Proposal* Swift has much less room to move, and he has therefore to work faster. The gradual approach would never do here. His method in *A Modest Proposal* is to deaden our sensitivity at the very outset, by anaesthetising whole areas of our consciousness. His procedure here bears a considerable resemblance to what takes place when we visit our dentist to have a tooth stopped. We listen at first to some easy, neutral conversation when we have seated ourselves in the chair. 'It is a melancholy object', we are told, 'to those who walk through this great town or travel in the country, when they see the streets, the roads, and cabin doors, crowded with beggars of the female sex, followed by three, four, or six children, all in rags and importuning every passenger for an alms.' We may wonder why our dentist has chosen to open with that particular topic, but his remarks seem sensible enough, and we rather admire him for showing such human feelings. For some time he continues in the same conversational vein while he is preparing for the injection, and then comes the first tentative prick. 'It is true,' he observes suddenly, 'that a child just dropped from its dam may be supported by her milk for a solar year.' We felt that one; and a moment or two later there comes a second prick, not quite so sharp: 'I calculate there may be about 200,000 couple whose wives are breeders....' The cocaine is now beginning to work, but we are not yet ready for the drill. We must have one deeper injection, and it comes almost at once:

I have been assured by a very knowing American of my acquaintance in London, that a young healthy child well nursed is at a year old a most delicious, nourishing, and wholesome food, whether stewed, roasted, baked, or boiled; and I make no doubt that it will equally serve in a fricasee or a ragout. I do therefore humbly offer it to public consideration that of the 120,000 children already computed, 20,000 may be reserved for breed, whereof only one fourth part to be males.... That the remaining 100,000 may, at a year old, be offered in sale to the persons of quality and fortune through the kingdom; always advising the mother to let them suck plentifully in the last month, so as to render them plump and fat for a good table.

Swift can now start drilling as hard as he likes; for he has got us to accept his major premise that the Irish are treated no better than cattle by their English landlords, and, if that is really so, this proposal ought, as Swift suggests, to be 'very proper for the landlords, who, as they have already devoured most of the parents, seem to have the best title to the children.' In a short satire like the *Modest Proposal* the early stages are all-important, and Swift is a master at manœuvring his reader into a position which he would never voluntarily have taken up himself, but from which there is no escape until, like the wedding guest, he has heard the tale out to its bitter end.

In the prose satire of the eighteenth century Swift has no equal, but there are other respectable names. If satire is to be evaluated by its results, there have never been more successful satirists in English literature than Addison and Steele. They helped to educate their own generation, and to some extent effected a revolution in manners, and even morals. As a correspondent put it in *Spectator*, no. 461 (and we have no reason to suppose that this was one of those letters written to the editor by the editor himself): 'Your writings have made learning a more necessary part of good breeding than it was before you appeared;...modesty is become fashionable, and impudence stands in need of some wit since you have put them both in their proper lights. Profaneness, lewdness, and debauchery are not now qualifications, and a man may be a very fine gentleman tho' he is neither a keeper nor an infidel.' All this Addison and Steele effected by good-natured ridicule. Mr Bickerstaff ventured to tell the Town, as Gay put it, that 'they were a parcel of Fops, Fools, and vain Cocquets; but in such a manner, as even pleased them, and made them more than half enclin'd to believe that he spoke Truth.'[1] Their Horatian method of laughing men out of their follies and excesses differed from more drastic and downright methods as medical treatment differs from an operation. They had, too, what Swift had not, an organised and continually increasing public. Regular periodical publication enabled them to carry on a campaign, with all the attendant advantages of being able to follow up a topic until the particular folly disintegrated before their persistent ridicule.

Among the satires of the period no longer widely read, there is Arbuthnot's *History of John Bull*, too deeply imbedded in domestic and international politics to be of much interest today. A shorter piece of his, *The Art of Political Lying*, has acquired a new relevance in the twentieth century, and deserves to be better known. Pope's attack on Lord Hervey, *A Letter to a Noble Lord*, not published in his own lifetime, belongs to a vigorous minor genre that includes Defoe's *Reply to Lord Haversham* and Burke's *Letter to a Noble Lord*. Pope's *The Art of Sinking in Poetry* must be one of the few pieces of ironical criticism in the language, although early in the next century we have Bishop Copleston's delightful *Advice to a Young Reviewer*. All through the eighteenth century, too, in periodicals like *The Craftsman* and John Wilkes's *North Briton*, and of course in the celebrated *Letters of Junius*, we find political satire that often reaches a high standard. It would no doubt be a good deal less interesting if the writers had not been driven so frequently to allegory, fable, historical parallels, and many other devices to safeguard themselves from legal action by governments or individuals.

The century that followed was less willing to listen to the satirist. Like twentieth-century America Victorian England was in the middle of an age of expansion and business enterprise; it therefore tended to frown on those Jeremiahs like Matthew Arnold who refused to tell it that 'all was for the best in the best of all possible worlds', and it prided itself on having developed a vigorous and self-assertive community,

> Where seldom is heard a discouraging word,
> And the skies are not cloudy all day.

The words of John Ridd in *Lorna Doone* probably express the opinion of the average Victorian reader:

> For it strikes me that of all human dealings, satire is the very lowest, and most mean and common. It is the equivalent in words for what bullying is in deeds; and no more bespeaks a clever man than the other does a brave one. These two wretched tricks exalt a fool in his own esteem, but never in his neighbour's; for the deep common sense of our nature tells us that no man of a genial heart, or of any spread of mind, can take pride in either.[1]

Yet the nineteenth century produced one remarkable satirist, the author of *Erewhon*. Like Byron, Samuel Butler had consciously separated himself from the great majority of his fellow-countrymen, and he could view the Victorian age almost as an outsider. He had quarrelled with his family, he had taken himself off to New Zealand at the age of twenty-three to be a sheep farmer, and when he returned to London five years later he lived a semi-Bohemian life in bachelor's quarters in Staples Inn, varied by frequent visits to the Continent. He was not a social outcast by any means, and he was saved from mere bitterness by a lively sense of humour and by one or two close friendships. But he was isolated, and a certain amount of isolation is favourable to the satirist. Butler's laborious originality rather reminds one of those pavement artists who write 'All my own work' in coloured chalk at the head of their pictures. Among English satirists he has the same hard-working efficiency and something of the same clever but rather obvious invention that we find in Ben Jonson. If Butler lacked many of Byron's natural gifts he had thought much harder, and his satire on contemporary English life and habits is sometimes more penetrating. His biographer Festing Jones tells us that Butler often spoke of his own unimaginativeness.[1] He certainly had an odd way of working into his books actual incidents from his own life or the lives of others, and, in *The Way of all Flesh*, letters from his father or from other relatives. We are told that the judge's summing-up in the Erewhonian trial of the young man who was accused of pulmonary consumption ('an offence', says Butler, 'which was punished with death until quite recently') was lifted almost verbatim from a newspaper report of a man found guilty of theft.[1] I do not suggest that Butler was unique in thus working the actual into the fictional, but I doubt if this form of literary montage has ever been carried so far. Butler, I suspect, was always more concerned to make his satirical points, by any method whatever, than to stand upon any false pride of authorship. Much of his satire remains surprisingly relevant. In the chapters in *Erewhon* called 'The Colleges of Unreason', where he is dealing with our older universities, he remarks upon how the professors will rarely commit themselves to a definite opinion, from the suspicion that they might give themselves away.

As there is hardly any subject on which this suspicion cannot arise, I found it difficult to get definite opinions from any of them, except on such subjects as the weather, eating and drinking, holiday excursions, or games of skill.

If they cannot wriggle out of expressing an opinion of some sort, they will commonly retail those of someone who has already written on the subject, and conclude by saying that though they quite admit there is an element of truth in what the writer has

said, there are many points on which they are unable to agree
with him. Which these points were, I invariably found myself
unable to determine; indeed, it seemed to be counted the perfection of scholarship and good breeding among them not to have
—much less to express—an opinion on any subject on which it
might prove later that they had been mistaken. The art of sitting
gracefully on a fence has never, I should think, been brought to
greater perfection than at the Erewhonian Colleges of Unreason.[1]

Of twentieth-century satirists none has been more effective within his own carefully limited range than the late
Sir Max Beerbohm. To mention his name immediately after
that of Samuel Butler will at least serve to show how varied
English satire is, and how hard it is to define. If I were
giving a dinner party in Elysium I should certainly not place
Max Beerbohm anywhere near Samuel Butler. I should
prefer to seat Jane Austen on one side of him and Miss Ivy
Compton Burnett on the other, and the three would get
along beautifully. Max Beerbohm's satire is more a matter
of tone and atmosphere than of the palpable hit; it seems to
originate in a fastidious distaste for excess, extravagance,
over-emphasis, crudity, absurdity—for anything that dis-
turbs his own delicately adjusted balance and his own poised
normality; and it is conveyed to us by a style which expresses
the subtlest shades of irony and the gentlest shrugs of
protest. If Max does not invariably adopt a *persona*, the
writer, as we soon realise, is often not quite Max himself,
but an altogether simpler and more innocent personality
who enables him to make his points, and who is to Max
pretty much what Dr Watson is to Sherlock Holmes.

We can see his delicate malice at work on the literary
nonentities he deals with in *Seven Men*—on Enoch Soames,
the Decadent poet who was so unaccountably ignored by

Mr Holbrook Jackson in his critical study, *The Eighteen-Nineties*. ('I looked eagerly in the index for SOAMES, ENOCH. I had feared he would not be there. He was not there. But everybody else was.') The impossible Soames had published a slim volume of verse called *Fungoids*, but it had failed to make the faintest ripple on the literary world of the day. 'I looked out for what the metropolitan reviewers would have to say', Max tells us with the calm impartiality of the historian:

> They seemed to fall into two classes: those who had little to say and those who had nothing. The second class was the larger, and the words of the first were cold; insomuch that
>
> Strikes a note of modernity throughout.... These tripping numbers.
> —*Preston Telegraph*

was the sole lure offered in advertisements by Soames's publisher.

This is bad enough; but on the next page Max gives another turn to the screw. 'I learned afterwards', he observes casually,

> that he was the son of an unsuccessful and deceased book-seller in Preston, but had inherited an annuity of £300 from a married aunt, and had no surviving relatives of any kind. Materially, then, he was 'all right'. But there was still a spiritual pathos about him, sharpened for me now by the possibility that even the praises of 'The Preston Telegraph' might not have been forth-coming had he not been the son of a Preston man.

So poor Soames dissolves into the wraith he is before our eyes, reduced by the pitiless sympathy of Max to a final ignominy.

The satire of Sir Max Beerbohm played easily upon the minor follies and affectations and absurdities of life. That of George Orwell was concerned with the major political issues of the twentieth century, and indeed with the future of human civilisation. In so far as he can be defined in one word Orwell was a Liberal, and like other Liberals with high hopes for humanity he had begun by welcoming the Russian Revolution, and had then seen it going all wrong. In *Animal Farm* he is therefore with the animals against Farmer Brown, but he is against Snowball and Napoleon and Squealer and the other pigs who have taken control of the Revolution on the farm and are now running it in their own interest. Orwell pursues his satirical theme with an unfailing relevance and at times with a sort of grim geniality, but the prevailing note is one of sadness, a sadness that is not uncommon in fairy tales and that here reflects an awareness of how easily things go wrong. One feels all through this beast fable his pity for the animals who set out so hopefully to build a better society, and whose good will and hard work were exploited by the unscrupulous for their own ends. The real hero of *Animal Farm* is old Boxer, the enormous cart-horse standing almost eighteen hands high, who has been decorated for his bravery with the order of Animal Hero, First Class, and who works himself to a premature death by his devoted labour on the farm. Nothing that Orwell had written before 1945 suggested that he had the discipline and the literary finesse for a satire of this kind; but here in *Animal Farm* he comes near to Swift in the grave, controlled way in which he tells his story, and the sureness with which he turns the imaginary situation to account and presses home his satire. It is so easy in this form of writing to slide into the facetious or extravagant, to be too obvious or too obscure; but Orwell never makes a mistake.

In some ways *Nineteen Eighty-Four* is a more powerful work; it attacks totalitarianism at more points than *Animal*

Farm, and it has passages of great satirical ingenuity. All that Orwell has to say about the Ministry of Love and the Ministry of Truth, about Big Brother and the Two Minutes Hate and Newspeak, is highly effective. In *Nineteen Eighty-Four*, too, he succeeded at times in being thoroughly frightening. He wanted to warn and admonish, to compel his own generation to take notice of what he believed to be a monstrous evil, and his shock treatment was undeniably successful. That he based his vision of the future on war-time London, with its restrictions and shortages and general run-down appearance, was fair enough; his world of 1984 is a world perpetually at war, controlled by a political regime for which propaganda and secret police and economic hardship for the masses are the permanent and necessary conditions of survival. In this book Orwell has created a sort of inverted Utopia, a world run on hatred and lies and oppression, and anything that will darken his picture is relevant to his purpose. But if so successful a book can be said to fail, it fails because its situations and symbols are too contrived. *Nineteen Eighty-Four* is to *Animal Farm* as *A Voyage to Laputa* is to *A Voyage to Lilliput*; the points are made, but the objective correlatives are constructed rather than discovered. *Nineteen Eighty-Four* has neither the inevitability nor the imaginative certainty of Orwell's one unique and perfect work, *Animal Farm*.

V

THE NOVEL

THE satirical novel is a comparatively minor genre, and has never, perhaps, had a wide popular appeal. From the time of Henry Fielding, however, incidental satire has been an important ingredient in English fiction. 'Of all kinds of satire,' Smollett wrote in the preface to *Roderick Random*, 'there is none so entertaining, and universally improving, as that which is introduced, as it were occasionally, in the course of an interesting story.' In considering the satire which appears 'as it were occasionally' in English novels, we may find once again that it is not always easy to distinguish satire from comedy, but the distinction can usually be made, and with some novelists is quite unmistakable. It happens very conveniently that Fielding provides us with examples of both formal and occasional satire: *The Life of Mr Jonathan Wild the Great* may be looked upon as our first purely satirical novel, and there are many satirical passages scattered through Fielding's other novels.

The importance of Samuel Richardson in the satirical development of Fielding has always been recognised; it was Fielding's dislike of Richardson's moral values that prompted him first of all to write the crude and hilarious, but severely damaging *Shamela*, in which, to quote from the long descriptive title, 'all the matchless Arts of that young Politician [are] set in a true and just Light', and then, some months later, to follow it up with *The History and Adventures of Joseph Andrews*. It is customary to say that, while *Joseph Andrews* begins as a sort of parody of *Pamela*, Fielding soon becomes so interested in his own story that he almost forgets his serious disagreement with Richardson's view of life and all that it implied. But Richardson was to Fielding pretty much what the Victorians were to Lytton Strachey, at once a congenial theme and a source of provocation, and while Fielding was writing *Joseph Andrews* Richardson's moral assumptions were constantly present in his mind. He was still conscious of them, or of views similar to them, when he was writing *Tom Jones*. It must not be forgotten that Richardson had a large and enthusiastic following; almost everyone had read, or was reading, *Pamela*, and nearly everyone approved of it. To Fielding, who believed that Richardson's morality was very much a matter of 'Let's pretend', and that in consequence he was giving his readers a false picture of life and an idea of virtue that would never stand up to the wear and tear of reality, Richardson was a proper target for the darts of satire. Fielding repeatedly claimed that in his own prose fiction he was writing what he called 'history', and that in creating his characters his aim had been to draw his materials from human nature only, to record the truth. That is, on the whole, what he succeeded in doing, and if it had not been for Richardson he might have done no more than that. If the influence of Richardson on him is imponderable, it is always there, and it helps to account, I imagine, for Fielding's habit of trailing his coat, for a certain challenging air in his account of men and women. He was continually aware of false values to be exposed, of the need not merely to tell the truth about men and women, but to demonstrate that what passed for truth in the writings of Richardson and others like him was in fact make-believe and pretence.

An outraged sense of truth is therefore responsible for a good deal of Fielding's satire, and may sometimes force him into apparently taking a lower view of average humanity than the facts would seem to warrant. A good example of Fielding at work is the well-known scene in *Joseph Andrews*[1] where Joseph having been beaten and stripped by robbers is left lying naked and half-dead in the ditch. Fielding now develops the situation:

> The poor wretch, who lay motionless a long time, just began to recover his senses as a stage-coach came by. The postilion hearing a man's groans, stopped his horses, and told the coachman, he was certain there was a dead man lying in the ditch, for he heard him groan. 'Go on, sirrah,' says the coachman, 'we are confounded late, and have no time to look after dead men.' A lady, who heard what the postilion said, and likewise heard the groan, called eagerly to the coachman to stop and see what was the matter. Upon which he bid the postilion alight, and look into the ditch. He did so, and returned, 'That there was a man sitting upright, as naked as ever he was born.'—'O J——sus!' cried the lady; 'A naked man! Dear coachman, drive on and leave him.'

Fielding is now ready for one of his favourite literary gambits, the formal development of a satirical theme. Each of the travellers in the coach is stripped as naked spiritually as poor Joseph has been physically; the fine lady's false delicacy, the old gentleman's cowardly selfishness, the equally selfish lawyer's professional cautiousness are all exposed in turn. 'Robbed,' cries the old gentleman. 'Let us make all the haste imaginable, or we shall be robbed too.' But the young lawyer, who heartily wished they had passed by without taking any notice, points out that 'now they might be proved to have been last in his company; if he should die they might be called to some account for his murder. He therefore thought it advisable to save the poor creature's life, for their own sakes, if possible; at least, if he died, to prevent the jury's finding that they fled for it.' So it is agreed that Joseph must be taken into the coach. But the lady still protests that she would 'rather stay in that place to all eternity, than ride with a naked man'. At this point she receives unexpected support from the coachman, who declares that 'he could not suffer him to be taken in, unless somebody would pay a shilling for his carriage the four miles'. The argument inevitably begins all over again, but finally the lawyer, who is of course thinking exclusively of what might happen to himself if Joseph should die, frightens the coachman into taking Joseph up. But now comes an entirely new complication. As Joseph advances towards the coach he catches sight of the lady, and absolutely refuses to enter the coach unless he is given something to cover himself with, to avoid offering any offence to decency. 'So perfectly modest was this young man,' Fielding explains, and then, with one of his most delightful strokes of irony, 'such mighty effects had the spotless example of the amiable Pamela, and the excellent sermons of Mr Adams, wrought upon him.' No wonder Richardson loathed Fielding.

All that is needed is for someone to lend Joseph a great-coat (there were several lying about in the coach); but the two gentlemen find that they are cold and can't spare theirs, and the coachman, who is sitting on two, refuses to lend one of his for fear it should be made bloody. The lady's footman 'desired to be excused for the same reason, which the lady herself, notwithstanding her abhorrence of a naked man, approved'. Human nature is vindicated at last by the postilion, 'a lad', says Fielding, rubbing in a little more salt, 'who hath since been transported for robbing a henroost', and who now 'voluntarily stripped off a great-coat, his only garment, at the same time swearing a great oath (for which he was rebuked by the passengers), that "he would rather ride in his shirt all his life, than suffer a fellow-creature to lie in so miserable a condition".'

This is surely one of the great moments in English satire. It is characteristic of Fielding (as it would have been of Dickens in the same circumstances) that the Good Samaritan is the poorest person in the company. Of the others involved, the coachman comes nearest to having some vestiges of humanity; Fielding goes so far as to admit that the coachman consents to take up Joseph because he was 'perhaps a little moved to compassion at the poor creature's condition, who stood bleeding and shivering with the cold'. The others think only of themselves. All through there is a clear and determined contrast between natural human feeling and utter heartlessness, or between natural feelings and the artificial, affected feelings of the refined. If Richardson had been travelling in that coach, we may hope, and even believe, that he would have acted with humanity; but he would certainly have rebuked the postilion when he swore his great oath, and if he had learnt later of the lad's having been transported for robbing a henroost he would probably have reflected that it was no more than he had expected. Fielding's handling of the whole episode no doubt verges on the obvious—it has, at least, the formal pattern of eighteenth-century art—and yet the situation is exploited with a beautiful sense of timing and with a nice judgment of what will constitute the last straw, which he may have learnt from his long experience as a playwright.

The scene near the end of the novel,[1] where Parson Adams is told that his son Jacky has been drowned, may again be rather obviously planned, but again the obviousness is concealed by the zest with which Fielding develops the situation. Adams has been rebuking Joseph for his unseemly impatience to be married to his adorable Fanny:

You are a young man, and can know but little of this world; I am older, and have seen a great deal. All passions are criminal in their excess; and even love itself, if it is not subservient to our duty, may render us blind to it. Had Abraham so loved his son Isaac, as to refuse the sacrifice required, is there any of us who would not condemn him? Joseph, I know your many good qualities, and value you for them; but, as I am to render an account of your soul, which is committed to my cure, I cannot see any fault without reminding you of it. You are too much inclined to passion, child, and have set your affections so absolutely on this young woman, that if God required her at your hands, I fear you would reluctantly part with her. Now, believe me, no Christian ought so to set his heart on any person or thing in this world, but that, whenever it shall be required, or taken from him in any manner by divine Providence, he may be able, peaceably, quietly, and contentedly to resign it.

It was just at this point that a message reached Parson Adams that his youngest son had been drowned. For a moment he stood silent, and then gave way to a passion of grief. Joseph, who was almost as distressed as Adams, tried in every way he knew to comfort him, using some of the arguments that he remembered from the parson's own discourses, 'for he was a great enemy to the passions, and preached nothing more than the conquest of them by reason and grace'. But Adams was not to be comforted.

'Child, child,' said he, 'do not go about impossibilities. Had it been any other of my children, I could have borne it with patience; but my little prattler, the darling and comfort of my old age—the little wretch, to be snatched out of life just at his entrance into it; the sweetest, best-tempered boy, who never did a thing to offend me....'

Fielding is now getting into his stride:

'My poor Jacky, shall I never see thee more?' cries the parson.

'Yes, surely,' says Joseph, 'and in a better place, you will meet again, never to part more!'

I believe the parson did not hear these words, for he paid little regard to them, but went on lamenting, whilst the tears trickled down into his bosom. At last he cried out, 'Where is my little darling?' and was sallying out, when, to his great surprise and joy, in which I hope the reader will sympathise, he met his son, in a wet condition indeed, but alive, and running towards him. The person who brought the news of his misfortune had been a little too eager, as people sometimes are, from, I believe, no very good principle, to relate ill news; and seeing him fall into the river, instead of running to his assistance, directly ran to acquaint his father of a fate which he had concluded to be inevitable, but whence the child was relieved by the same poor pedlar who had relieved his father before from a less distress. The parson's joy was now as extravagant as his grief had been before; he kissed and embraced his son a thousand times, and danced about the room like one frantic....

Is this comedy or satire? What lies behind the episode is partly Fielding's perception (which he shared with Swift) of the way in which a man's profession is apt to become the man himself: the lawyer remains a lawyer, not merely when he is in his office but when he is in his bed or in his bath. So, too, with doctors, parsons, and every other profession and trade. Like Swift, Fielding much preferred 'John, Peter, Thomas, and so forth' to the stereotype which we are all in danger of becoming. In his lengthy homily to Joseph, the parson has been behaving professionally, using the jargon of his profession, inculcating principles which are probably impracticable, and which in any case he cannot live up to himself. And then Fielding suddenly shows us the real man. He is smiling at Adams, of course, but he thoroughly approves his lapse from those standards that he has been trying to impress upon Joseph. Adams was in danger of becoming a mere sounding-board for moral precepts; he has now proved his common humanity. It is not therefore the parson (a naturally good man) who is the main target of Fielding's satire, but those who suppose that the goodness inculcated by preaching and virtuous maxims is ever likely to stand up to the test of real life. And to Fielding the most notorious of those well-meaning moralists was Samuel Richardson. It is Richardson's morality that is exposed in the failure of Parson Adams, in a moment of crisis, to benefit from his own impeccable principles.*

Jonathan Wild is a brilliant and sustained performance, but I must add the damaging reservation that no one ever wished it longer. The satirical idea of the book becomes a little monotonous. As W. P. Ker once remarked, 'One wishes to end it; the jury does not desire to hear more'.[1] *Jonathan Wild*, in fact, raises in an acute form the question of how long one can endure unmitigated satire. In most extended satires, such as *Gulliver's Travels* or *Erewhon*, there is a good deal of relief offered by the narrative itself, and by incidents and descriptions that are not closely related

---

* The chapter heading for this episode, 'A discourse which happened between Mr Adams, Mrs Adams, Joseph, and Fanny; with some behaviour of Mr Adams, which will be called by some few readers very low, absurd, and unnatural', seems again to be directed against Richardson.

to the satirical purpose. Fielding's narrative has considerable interest; it is the tone of sustained irony, the continued insistence on the theme of the great man and the low grovelling nature of the virtuous Heartfree, that becomes monotonous.

There is a good deal of satire in the novels of Smollett, and there is some quite startling satire of middle-class vulgarity in Fanny Burney's *Evelina*. Few passages in English fiction make one feel so embarrassed as those in which Fanny Burney presents the appalling Branghton family in action. This is very nearly satire by direct mimicry, for Miss Burney had a remarkable ear for the accent and idiom of English speech; and yet one wonders whether some of the embarrassment is not due to a feeling that Evelina herself is really a frightful little snob, and that her creator who so evidently approves of her must also be suspect. Satire by direct mimicry is no doubt an inaccurate description of what is happening with the Branghton family; they are the satirical creation of a fastidious young lady, and she must be given full credit for it. But the Branghtons are clearly, too, the result of close and pained observation of such people in real life. To satirise vulgarity it is hardly necessary to do more than give it expression in accurate dialogue.

The border line between satire and unsatirical good sense and good taste is often hard to draw. That this should be so suggests that stupidity and ignorance and extravagance are so widespread that merely to see clearly and speak the truth is enough to make most people think that you are being sharp and satirical and disillusioned. Yet there is no question of disillusionment with such a writer as Jane Austen. She has not lost her illusions, because she never had any, and what may seem satirical is often no more than her habitually precise discrimination. We are always conscious with her, as we are with the less subtle Fielding, of the poised and critical author, prepared to react satirically if the occasion should call for satire, but for the most part regarding her characters and their actions with a singularly clear and undisturbed vision. When a satirical comment is called for in Jane Austen's novels it sometimes comes from the author herself, but is perhaps more often put into the mouth of one of her characters, where at one and the same time it establishes the critical attitude required, and reinforces that impression of good sense and intelligence which that character is intended to make upon us.

Historians of prose fiction have suggested that one of the literary influences on the development of the novel was the character sketch so frequently written in the seventeenth century. By their steady concentration upon the precise definition of their various types, the character writers must have contributed a good deal towards the satirical delineation of character. We can see the importance of this psychological analysis in the following character sketch:

A plain honest fellow is one that to avoid one kind of affectation falls into another. Because he believes many people pretend to more admiration of the beauties of nature than they really feel, and is disgusted with such pretensions, he affects greater indifference and less discrimination in viewing them himself than he possesses. He is fastidious and will have an affectation of his own.

That passage comes, not from a seventeenth-century 'character', but from *Sense and Sensibility*,[1] and though I have tampered with it so as to conceal its origin, the only alteration I had to make was in the opening sentence, which runs: 'I suspect', said Elinor, 'that to avoid one kind of affectation, Edward here falls into another.' Elinor Dashwood is speaking—Elinor, the clear-sighted and discriminating elder sister—and her comment is occasioned by the insistence of Edward Ferrars that he is a man of plain tastes, and not fine enough to understand the picturesque, as the hypersensitive Marianne does. In the novel, of course, the passage serves to illuminate the characters of all three. The gentle satire on Marianne's romantic sensibility and the difference between the two sisters are expressed again in Edward's next observation to Marianne:

'I am convinced', said Edward, 'that you really feel all the delight in a fine prospect which you profess to feel. But, in return, your sister must allow me to feel no more than I profess. I like a fine prospect, but not on picturesque principles. I do not like crooked, twisted, blasted trees. I admire them much more if they are tall, straight, and flourishing. I do not like ruined, tattered cottages. I am not fond of nettles, or thistles, or heath blossoms. I have more pleasure in a snug farm-house than a watch-tower—and a troop of tidy, happy villagers please me better than the finest banditti in the world.'

Marianne looked with amazement at Edward, with compassion at her sister. Elinor only laughed.[1]

Sense and Sensibility lacks something of the subtlety of Jane Austen's later novels. The scene at the beginning of the book[2] where the mean and selfish John Dashwood is gradually persuaded by his equally ungenerous wife that his feeling of obligation to his stepmother is excessive, until in the end he is convinced that he will have performed all that can be reasonably expected of him if he helps her to move her furniture, is undeniably effective, and might with very few changes have come out of a novel by Fielding; but the lines are—for Jane Austen—rather too heavily drawn. Yet to find anything that we could call crude in her work we have to turn to the satirical stories which she wrote in her teens. *Love and Freindship*, with its romantic-egoist heroine Laura, offers no real basis for comparison with *Sense and Sensibility*; it is, in fact, a hilarious skit. 'Never,' Laura tells Marianne, 'never did I see such an affecting Scene as was the meeting of Edward and Augustus....It was too pathetic for the feelings of Sophia and myself. We fainted alternately on a sofa.'[1] That represents fairly enough the burlesque tone of *Love and Freindship* (a remarkable performance, incidentally, for a girl of fifteen). Yet, even in this early piece, subtlety will keep breaking in, and we become aware of that cool intelligence that was to preside over all her mature writing. 'Lovely as I was,' Laura confides to her correspondent, 'the Graces of my Person were the least of my Perfections.... In my Mind, every Virtue that could adorn it was centred: it was the Rendez-vous of every good Quality and of every noble sentiment. A sensibility too tremblingly alive to every affliction of my Freinds, my Acquaintance and particularly to every affliction of my own, was my only fault, if fault it could be called.'[2] In that phrase, 'and particularly to every affliction of my own', the young satirist is already beginning to show her quality, that quiet and barely perceptible thinning of the smile which marks her transition from the comic to the satirical.

Sooner or later we must face the question whether the satirical vision does not impose a severe limitation on the novelist, and we could not do better than look for an answer to that question in the novels of Jane Austen. It may be argued that the satirist is unable to create complete characters who respond freely to events and circumstances, because he is too much committed to his own satirical interpretation. He does not see the man or the woman, it may be said, but the particular folly or moral imperfection which is their dominant quality, and which it has become his business to demonstrate every time those characters appear. Thus Marianne is sensibility carried to excess; Mr Collins is insensitive self-importance; Mrs Elton is a social climber; Sir Walter Elliot is a snob, and so on. This objection cannot be easily brushed aside. The satirist almost invariably tends to simplify, and what he gains in clearness and emphasis he is apt to lose in complexity. Very little is lost, however, when (as is usually the case) the characters who are most consistently viewed from a satirical angle are the minor figures in the novel. There is almost no loss of naturalness, for we all tend to form rather simplified impressions of the casual acquaintances we meet on the morning train, or in the course of our day's work. We need not view them satirically, but unless something rather unusual happens we probably continue to look upon them as if they were minor characters in an unwritten novel, and not complex and individual human personalities. The older novelists, with their strong sense of perspective and formal pattern, tend to keep their background characters in the background; their minor characters do not suddenly come forward to lay bare their inmost feelings and so compete for our attention with Elizabeth Bennet or Emma or Anne Elliot. In the twentieth-century novel one can never be sure that some quiet character whom one had confidently relegated to the neutral background will not suddenly embarrass one, like a complete stranger in a railway carriage, with the most intimate revelations, and so step noisily into the foreground. The satirical novelist, then, is doing no harm if he views his minor characters with the detachment of the satirist; the danger comes when he sees one of his major characters in a satirical light. In *Sense and Sensibility* I don't think Jane Austen quite escapes criticism. In the early chapters Marianne is too much a figure of fun. It is excellent fun, but we hardly take Marianne seriously enough, and it is not until she is betrayed by Willoughby that she becomes a woman of real importance. Elizabeth Bennet is seen with complete sympathy from start to finish, and so too is Anne Elliot in *Persuasion*. Jane Austen's real triumph in the satirical portrayal of a heroine seems to me to be Emma.

I have just said that both Elizabeth Bennet and Anne Elliot are sympathetic portraits. Is the absence of sympathy, which one usually associates with the satirical attitude, fatal to the understanding and presentation of human character? It might be a sufficient answer to point out that the sympathy of a novelist with the creatures of his own imagination and his sympathy with them as moral beings are two quite distinct things, and that if Shakespeare, as Keats suggested,[1] took as much delight in conceiving an Iago as an Imogen, so could Jane Austen. But if this is thought an inadequate answer, or no answer at all, then I would reply that with Jane Austen it is not a question of sympathy on the one hand and a satirical withholding of sympathy on the other, but of every shade of mingled sympathy and satire. Emma Woodhouse is as completely realised as any character in English fiction, and yet her creator is fully alive to the imperfections in her character, and expresses them with a delicate satire that still leaves her free to explore the hidden springs of Emma's personality. So little, indeed, is the prevailingly satirical atmosphere in Jane Austen's novels a limiting factor that it does more than anything else to preserve them in a condition of eternal freshness.

I come now to a writer who presents a special problem, Thomas Love Peacock. Peacock has never been widely read, and the main reason for his lack of popular appeal is no doubt his failure to provide his readers with an interesting story, or indeed one that can be said to matter at all. But even among those readers, fit though few, who could do without the story, there are probably some who are antagonised by Peacock because they are unable to see just where he stands. There is no necessity at all for satire to be always deadly obvious. Yet we ought to be able to place a satirist without too much difficulty, and when we find so discerning a critic as Professor Louis Cazamian complaining of Peacock that 'the unity of his nature, the permanent axis of his mind, are not very easily discernible',[1] we must be prepared to admit that he presents his own special difficulty. The difficulty is roughly similar to that which we encounter with an independent member of parliament. An intelligent man may well feel unable to subscribe wholeheartedly to the policies of any one of the major political parties; he will make his own private synthesis. But just as in politics the action of the independent member is often unpredictable, and the plain man finds it hard to see what he is getting at, so with Peacock there seems to be no consistent attitude to the modern world. His satire plays impartially on progress and conservatism, on romanticism and rationalism. Among English satirists he is the floating vote, claiming the privilege to decide for himself about national education, competitive examinations, the march of mind, modern science, Shelley,

America, and much else. Perhaps of all his numerous characters the one who comes nearest to Peacock himself is Dr Folliott of *Crotchet Castle*, who appears to be against all the other guests, and who might well have anticipated Oscar Wilde's remark, 'When people agree with me I always feel that I must be wrong'. Ultimately the unity that Professor Cazamian is seeking is to be found only in Peacock's personality, and to enjoy Peacock all the time one must like him well enough to accept that personality without reserve. Mr J. B. Priestley's humorous description of him as 'an aristocratic individualistic republican Radical with a strong Tory bias, whose good pleasure it was to be always against the Government'[1] is probably as near a definition as we can get. But if that is a perfectly credible position for an individual Englishman to take up, it offered a very narrow and personal basis from which to satirise contemporary life. When a reader finds himself asking a satirist, 'What is it you *do* believe in?' there is perhaps some failure in the satire. We ought to be conscious that his victims have failed to measure up to certain implied standards, and if we are puzzled as to what those standards actually are we may resist or reject the satire.

I have already suggested that the Victorian reader was not particularly fond of satire, but in fact he got a good deal of it from his novelists, and either put up with it, or else, when he felt that it could not be applied to himself, presumably enjoyed it. With Dickens, as with Shakespeare, satire is only one of the many stops in his organ, to be pulled out occasionally. His novels move from one kind of effect to another, and the principle of unity (apart from an elaborate plot) is Dickens himself—the strong Dickens atmosphere, as penetrating and widespread as a London fog. When Dickens is satirical, it will usually be found that he is attacking the calculating, the prudent, the respectable, the pompous, the hard-hearted, the selfish, the hypocrite—the Veneerings, Mr Dombey, Mr Podsnap, Mr Pecksniff, and so on. In this he stands very much where Fielding stood with his Blifils and Squares and Thwackums. I have to add that he is apt to satirise what he knows only superficially and from the outside; the Circumlocution Office is good fun in its way, but it is not really seen from the inside, as is Mr Dorrit in the Marshalsea.

Mr Dorrit is one of Dickens's most remarkable studies in character. Ordinarily Dickens has a kindly feeling for this sort of man (Mr Micawber, after all, is another of the same kind); he can usually find quite a lot of good in him, and the faults are those of weakness, not of assurance and of hard, cold arrogance. We might therefore expect Mr Dorrit to get off lightly. But although he is not insensitive Mr Dorrit has the appalling egotism and selfishness that often go with sensitiveness, and as his position in the Marshalsea becomes more assured he steadily deteriorates. He is the hero of his own play, and like all great actors he dominates the world he moves in. This uncrowned King of the Marshalsea is a sort of plebeian Richard II; everything is as he sees or feels it to be, everything is viewed in its relationship to himself. Dickens has given us in William Dorrit a piercing analysis of a self-deception that is not always as respectable as genuine self-deception, and often amounts to a deliberate shutting of his eyes to what he knows he would find if he chose to look. His wrath with Little Dorrit when he sees her walking arm in arm with old Nandy, and the later scene where he rounds on young John who has brought a box of cigars to him at his hotel are ghastly revelations of human pride and wrong-headedness.

Why, then, is Dickens so much harder on Mr Dorrit than on Mr Micawber? Partly, no doubt, because of this pride in his respectable origin that Mr Dorrit clings to, and that contrasts so painfully with the warm-heartedness of the many humble people who have befriended him in his adversity. But when Dickens takes a satirical view of one of his characters it is usually because that character has caused, or is causing, suffering and unhappiness to some other character of whom he approves; and this is very evidently so in *Little Dorrit*. If there were no Little Dorrit to suffer, Dickens might have drawn Mr Dorrit on purely comic lines. As it is, he shows up his faults without mercy. Still, he does not forget that what Mr Dorrit has become is partly due to the situation in which he is placed, and that his prison life has had a rotting effect on his character. And there was another factor that he had to take into account. Characters in fiction are not isolated units; they react upon each other, and modify our impressions of those other characters with whom they come in contact. If Mr Dorrit were made a monster, our opinion of Little Dorrit would suffer; there must be some basis for her deep love and self-sacrifice. In this novel, however, Dickens has achieved a satirical study of a major character which leaves Mr Dorrit astonishingly real and quite painfully humiliating.

With Thackeray we arrive at a novelist in whose work satire is much more prevalent, but in whom satire is notoriously mixed with sentiment. 'If there is any exhibition in all Vanity Fair,' Thackeray once wrote, 'which Satire and

Sentiment can visit arm in arm together; where you light on the strangest contrasts laughable and tearful...' it is at an auction sale of household goods.[1] Thackeray's own habitual attitude is balanced (not, I think, precariously, because the attitude is natural to him) between the satirical and the sentimental. The effect is one of shot silk, gin and bitters, grapefruit and sugar. We accept this from Thackeray (at least I hope we do) because he is not blundering clumsily from the one to the other, but writing from a point of view that gives full scope to both. When, as in *Barry Lyndon*, he tries the sustained irony of Fielding's *Jonathan Wild* he is much less successful. In *Vanity Fair* he is tough-minded enough to make us believe that he is not giving way to facile feeling, and he has feeling enough to keep us from thinking him merely cynical. If we have any reservations it is surely not to the mixture of satire and sentiment as such, but to a suspicion that the bitters are sometimes better than the gin, and the grapefruit than the sugar. At least it is probably true to say that if it were not for the satirical and man-of-the-world side of Thackeray we should rather quickly find the sentiment too cloying.

Thackeray is less apt than Fielding and Dickens to find most of his good people among the poor and humble and his bad among the rich, but the influence of Fielding on Thackeray is not in doubt. To suggest how strong this influence was, I choose a passage from *Vanity Fair* (not at all an outstanding one), in which Thackeray is dealing with the last days of Sir Pitt Crawley. This old reprobate has now taken for his mistress the butler's daughter, Miss Betsy Horrocks, who has quickly got rid of almost all the staff. But there is one little kitchenmaid called Hester who is high in Betsy's favour because she always calls her 'My lady', and who is duly promoted for it. Thackeray gives us a fascinating glimpse of Betsy Horrocks singing atrociously at the piano, and the little maid 'wagging her head up and down, and crying, "Lor, Mum, 'tis bittiful"—just like a genteel sycophant in a real drawing-room'. When Sir Pitt finally drinks himself into a fatal illness, his relations force their way into the house, and catch Betsy red-handed in the act of opening an escritoire with a bunch of Sir Pitt's keys.

'Look at that, James and Mr Crawley', cried Mrs Bute, pointing at the scared figure of the black-eyed, guilty wench.

'He gave 'em me; he gave 'em me!' she cried....

'Are there no handcuffs?' Mrs Bute continued, stamping in her clogs. 'There used to be handcuffs. Where's the creature's abominable father?'

'He *did* give 'em me,' still cried poor Betsy; 'didn't he, Hester?'

But Hester has sized up the situation, and she knows that Betsy's reign is over.

'Law, Betsy, how could you go for to tell such a wicked story!' said Hester, the little kitchen-maid late on her promotion—'and to Madam Crawley, so good and kind, and his Rev'rince (with a curtsey) and you may search all *my* boxes, Mum, I'm sure, and here's my keys as I'm an honest girl though of pore parents and workhouse bred—and if you find so much as a beggarly bit of lace or a silk stocking out of all the gownds as *you've* had the picking of may I never go to Church agin.'

'Give up your keys, you hardened hussey', hissed out the virtuous little lady in the calash.

'And here's a candle, Mum, and if you please, Mum, I can show you her room, Mum, and the press in the housekeeper's room, Mum, where she keeps heaps and heaps of things, Mum', cried out the eager little Hester with a profusion of curtseys.[1]

Lest we should be in any doubt about the meanness of Hester, we get a final glimpse of her nursing old Sir Pitt, now a paralytic. When the kind-hearted Lady Jane appeared, the helpless old man would smile; when she went away, he would utter 'inarticulate deprecatory moans'.

> When the door shut upon her he would cry and sob, where-upon Hester's face and manner, which was always exceedingly bland and gentle while her lady was present, would change at once, and she would make faces at him, and clench her fist, and scream out, 'Hold your tongue, you stoopid old fool', and twirl away his chair from the fire which he loved to look at—at which he would cry more.[1]

Perhaps Fielding would have spared us this last scene, but the uninhibited exposure of hypocrisy is very much in his manner.

It is always touch-and-go with Thackeray. He might equally well have decided that Sir Pitt was to be nursed in his last illness by some perfectly devoted little orphan born in a workhouse, whose tender care would have been contrasted with the callous neglect of his own relatives. On some other occasion Thackeray might well have chosen to have it like that, because that was how he was feeling at the time. Here he wasn't, and so he doesn't. Ultimately the question with Thackeray must always be, what impression has he given of men and women when we have read the whole novel? In a novel called *Vanity Fair* we should naturally expect to find the worldly and the selfish predominating, but Thackeray also gives us Amelia and Dobbin and the O'Dowds and other kindly or worthy people. Conversely, the fairness of his satire can sometimes be seen when he is prepared to face the facts with a character whom he obviously admires. Even Dobbin's motives are closely scrutinised. It was he who had seen to it that George should marry Amelia. 'And why was it?' Thackeray asks.

Because he loved her so much that he could not bear to see her unhappy; or because his own sufferings of suspense were so unendurable that he was glad to crush them at once—as we hasten a funeral after a death, or, when a separation from those we love is imminent, cannot rest until the parting be over.[1]

With George Meredith we enter a world where satire has become so delicate that the traditional techniques of exaggeration and distortion have now almost given way to one of dispassionate exposure. The soul of Sir Willoughby Patterne in *The Egoist* is like a drop of water examined under the microscope, which is found to be swarming with amoebas and parameciums and other uncertain animalcula. The progressive revelation of the appalling egoism of Sir Willoughby is something that could be done only in the novel; it is effected partly by his composed and complacent conversation, and partly by the commentary of the author. Both are masterly; but so subtle are some of the indications of Sir Willoughby's personality that if Meredith had confined himself to the purely dramatic method of self-revelation his readers might sometimes have been in danger of missing the rarer significances. The commentary matches the dialogue in delicacy, and Meredith has the poet's ability to illuminate and define by the use of metaphor.

One of the finest passages in *The Egoist* is that in which Clara comes to realise the true nature of the man to whom she has allowed herself to become engaged.[2] The revelation is given gradually, but with a sense of growing horror. Sir Willoughby has wooed her and won her; he is a wealthy baronet, he has address and a fine presence, he seems to be generous, he talks well, and he has therefore impressed the young girl and carried her off from a crowd of admirers. (The capture, of course, is part of her attraction for Sir Willoughby.) But in the days that follow, Clara is slowly disenchanted; first one thing and then another awaken her doubts about him, and the doubt soon gives way to complete disillusionment. The man is an utter egoist. Worse still, he is an appalling bore. ('Certain is the vengeance of the young on monotony', Meredith tells us; 'nothing more certain.') Meredith brings the truth home to Clara, and to us his readers, with such consummate skill, that Sir Willoughby's unconscious self-exposure makes us actually uncomfortable; it is as if we had come round a corner in the grounds of Patterne Hall and found him putting on his underclothes after a swim in the lake.

He drew her hand more securely on his arm, to make her sensible that she leaned on a pillar of strength.

'Whenever the little brain is in doubt, perplexed, undecided which course to adopt, she will come to me, will she not? I shall always listen', he resumed soothingly....

And then, a few minutes later, he is speaking to her of his cousin Vernon. Vernon is a scholar, a poor relation whom Sir Willoughby has provided for and whom he patronises. ('Poor old Vernon', 'My dear good Vernon', and so on.) But Vernon has now decided to leave Patterne Hall, and try to live by his pen in London. Sir Willoughby is indignant. He is indignant because Vernon is his property, someone he has taken in hand, and therefore someone who is showing ingratitude by wishing to be independent.

'If he goes, he goes for good. It is the vital principle of my authority to insist on that. A dead leaf might as reasonably demand to return to the tree. Once off, off for all eternity! I am sorry, but such was your decision, my friend.'

'Is it fair to me,' Clara asks, 'that you should show me the worst of you?'

'All myself, my own?'

His ingratiating droop and familiar smile rendered 'All myself' so affectionately meaningful in its happy reliance upon her excess of love, that at last she understood she was expected to worship him and uphold him for whatsoever he might be, without any estimation of qualities; as indeed love does, or young love does: as she perhaps did once before he chilled her senses. That was before her 'little brain' had become active and had turned her senses to revolt.

It was on the full river of love that Sir Willoughby supposed the whole floating bulk of his personality to be securely sustained; and therefore it was that, believing himself swimming at his ease, he discoursed of himself.

It is my experience with Meredith that he is one of those authors who constantly provoke their readers to marginal comment. In library copies of his novels it is not uncommon to find words like 'Nonsense', 'Rubbish', and 'Not true' written in the margin, a sure indication that he has got under somebody's skin. I don't know that I have ever myself written in a Meredith margin, but I can still remember how, when I had read *The Egoist*, I was driven to gloomy self-examination, and how very uncomfortable Wilfrid Pole in *Emilia in England* made me feel—Wilfrid Pole who is so disconcerted when the lovely and fragile Emilia with whom he is falling in love insists on dwelling upon the fact that for weeks she had practically lived on potatoes.

The twentieth-century novel has added a good deal to English satire, but the biggest achievements of the novelists have lain elsewhere. At the beginning of the century appeared Samuel Butler's *The Way of All Flesh*, and so far as satire is concerned I think it remains the outstanding novel in this field. There are other satirical books, such as Norman Douglas's *South Wind*, and the early Peacock-like novels of Aldous Huxley, which are still being reprinted, read, and enjoyed, but it may be doubted that many of them will survive the century.

Satire, always hard to define, becomes still more difficult to isolate in an age in which the facts are so often presented with the sort of disenchanted actuality that we find in writers like Mr Kingsley Amis. But ultimately satire becomes inoperative if a writer's habitual attitude is one of expecting little or nothing of life and of his fellow men, and if he is unshockable because he has adopted a kind of moral nihilism, and has a mind so open that it positively yawns in the face of all human behaviour. Since the teaching of Freud became widely known, many factors have been at work which have deepened our knowledge of human personality, and have made the crude, simple judgments of the earlier satirists no longer adequate. But to find a psychoanalytical explanation of human aberrations is not to explain them away, and so long as we continue to form judgments of good and bad, right and wrong, the satirists will never be without employment.

VI

SATIRE IN THE THEATRE

SATIRE has always been unwelcome to people in authority; it is destructive, either of the individual, or of the party, or of the ideas and traditions on which established institutions are based. When it is personal it is perhaps most immediately dangerous in the theatre, for there its explosive qualities are greatly increased by the presence of an audience in whom excitement is easily generated. Readers are scattered up and down the country; an audience is concentrated in one place, and as the feelings of each individual are communicated to his neighbour the mass emotion may rapidly become overwhelming. Some sort of control over the theatre, therefore, has always been thought necessary, and it has been exercised in various ways, more or less satisfactory. By the close of the sixteenth century in England it was the duty of the Master of the Revels to satisfy himself that new plays should contain no matters of offence either to religion or to the government. He did so satisfy himself; but he sometimes made mistakes, and his censorship could never prevent the actors from introducing gags at any given performance.

In 1737, as a result mainly of Fielding's outspoken satire of Walpole and the Whig government, the Licensing Act was passed, and the control of the theatres was vested in the Lord Chamberlain acting on the advice of an official called the Licenser of Plays, now usually referred to as the Censor. The alternative to having a licenser is not necessarily complete licence. As Shaw and many others have argued, the stage could be regulated in the same way as the press, i.e. by subsequent prosecution where there is good cause to suppose that an offence has been committed. This is, in fact, the procedure in many other countries (for example, the United States), and it appears to work satisfactorily. But the English, who never willingly pull down an old building, however ugly and inconvenient, have clung to the censorship of plays, and have characteristically adapted it to purposes for which it was not originally intended

While the English drama was still in its infancy, satirical plays were fairly common; and for special reasons religious satire flourished in the sixteenth century. In the interludes of John Heywood those favourite butts of medieval satire, the Pardoner and the Friar, are often exposed to good-natured ridicule. Heywood's satire is that of a good Catholic who wishes that his Church were better; on the other hand, such Protestant plays as *Lusty Juventus* were written by those who wished it away altogether. During the troubled years of the sixteenth century when England went over to Protestantism under Henry VIII, remained Protestant under Edward VI, swung violently back to Roman Catholicism under Mary, and returned to Protestantism under Elizabeth, the drama was used by those in power to satirise alternately the Roman Catholic and the Protestant religion. With the accession of Queen Elizabeth the pendulum swung back rather less violently, but we are told that in the first Christmas of her reign 'the court and the streets were full of masks, in which cardinals, bishops, and abbots were held up to derision as crows, asses, and wolves'.[1] Elizabeth's aim, however, was to compose religious hatreds and rule over a united nation; and some Cambridge scholars gave great offence in 1564 when they insisted on entertaining her with a burlesque of the old religion. The Queen had been paying a visit to Cambridge (a stronghold of Puritanism), and had sat through two Latin plays and an English one on successive days. When on the fourth day she was invited to attend a Latin version of one of Sophocles' tragedies she signified that the royal patience was exhausted, and after polite farewells proceeded on her way to Hinchinbrook, the next stage in her progress. It was here that the disappointed scholars caught up with her and acted a crude burlesque of the Mass, which had apparently been intended as an afterpiece to the Sophocles play, and which they obviously felt was too good to be wasted.[1]

Those satirical interludes and masks are small fry compared with Sir David Lindsay's great dramatic 'flabberdabber', *Ane Satyre of the Thrie Estaits*, an astonishingly vigorous but amorphous satire. In a succession of robust and outspoken interludes he brings his reforming zeal to bear on the Lords, the Commons, and the Church, but chiefly on the Church. In spite of the iron curtain of Middle Scots that separates him from his twentieth-century reader, the satire still vibrates with much of its original power, and can still hold an audience, as was shown at the Edinburgh Festival some years ago. To the audience of 12 August 1554, consisting of the Queen Regent, a large part of the Scots nobility, and an exceeding great number of the common people, it must have come over with a tremendous impact. If its author died a Catholic, it can only have been because the Protestant creed in Scotland had not yet been definitely formulated. With Lindsay we are back in the days of outright invective, mixed with the sort of coarse, plain-spoken comedy that would have been appreciated by the Wife of Bath or by Dunbar's Tua Mariit Wemen and the Wedo. But the title-page of Robert Charteris's edition of 1602, 'Ane Satyre of the Thrie Estaits, in commendation of vertew and vituperation of vyce', should serve to remind us that, although in modern times satire is associated with ridicule and contempt, the word 'satire' was also used in classical times (as Dacier and Dryden pointed out) to describe that kind of writing which recommends virtue directly, as well as indirectly by implication.[1]

We are so used to thinking of the Elizabethan age as one in which it was dangerous to criticise or flout authority, that we may tend to underestimate the extent to which satire was possible in the Elizabethan theatre. During the Marprelate controversy the Puritans were, of course, fair game, and Lyly and Nashe were even encouraged to satirise them on the stage. So vigorous was the satire that Sir Edmund Chambers is able to say of this brief period that '*Vetus Comoedia*, the savage Aristophanic invective, was assuredly in full swing upon the English boards'.[2] Before long, however, authority clamped down again, and it was never safe to become too satirical in the theatre. Ben Jonson, for one, found himself several times in serious trouble. In the summer of 1597 he was committed to the Marshalsea for his share in *The Isle of Dogs*, and not released until October; in 1603 he had to appear before the Privy Council to answer a charge of popery and treason which the Earl of Northampton claimed to have found in *Sejanus*; and in 1605 he was in prison again for his part in *Eastward Ho!*, a play containing some mild satire of the Scots.

If a dramatist avoided religion and state matters (and if no officious person discovered allusions to them where none was intended), he was fairly free to breathe his satirical vein, and even to indulge in personalities. In the closing years of the sixteenth century, and the opening years of the seventeenth, the London playgoer was entertained by the quarrel of Ben Jonson with Marston and Dekker, the so-called war of the theatres, or *poetomachia*. Where so much honest doubt exists as to who exactly is being attacked, it can hardly be maintained that such plays as Jonson's *Every Man out of his Humour*, *Cynthia's Revels*, and *The Poetaster*, or Dekker's *Satiromastix*, have much that can interest us today. Writers for the theatre have always tended to live by taking in each other's washing, and have also, perhaps, shown more malice towards their rivals than other authors; a modern London revue will usually contain one or more sketches in which current plays are parodied or travestied, at once flattering the dramatic experience of the audience and scoring off a successful contemporary. Jonson has some good fun at Marston's expense, of course, and the scene near the end of *The Poetaster*,[1] where Crispinus is sick and brings up all sorts of hard words like 'glibbery', 'lubrical', 'turgidous', 'fatuate', has all Jonson's rough, it rather obvious, efficiency.

But he could do better than that. In *Every Man out of his Humour* he had put on the stage various contemptible characters—'a vain-glorious knight', 'a neat, spruce, affecting courtier', and so on—but he had satirised them more by description than in action. In calling this and the two plays that followed it 'comical satires' he almost suggested that they were dramatised extensions of the verse satire that was being written by his contemporaries, Hall and Marston.

Indeed, a good deal of the satire is put into the mouths of such commentators as Macilente and Carlo Buffone, who rail and snarl in the approved satirical fashion. But in his later plays, *Volpone*, *The Alchemist*, and *Bartholomew Fair*, Jonson satirises greed and credulity and hypocrisy by showing them in action, and so makes a much firmer bid for our attention. Volpone, Sir Epicure Mammon, Tribulation Wholesome, Ananias, Zeal-of-the-Land Busy, and the rest are not only condemned out of their own mouths, but they are involved in situations which are beautifully contrived to expose their sin and folly. Of the three plays I have just mentioned *Volpone* is the most consistently satirical; if we perhaps develop an unwilling admiration for the strength and cunning of Volpone, we are never left in any doubt about his wickedness, and at the end of the play he is haled off to prison, and Mosca is sent to the galleys. This is indeed what Sidney called 'the bitter, but wholesome iambick' which 'rubs the galled minde, in making shame the trumpet of villanie, with bolde and open crying out against naughtines'.[1] In comparison, the fate of the rogues in *The Alchemist* is mild indeed: Face, the double-crossing accomplice, emerges unscathed, with nothing but his conscience to punish him, and that is non-existent, while Subtle and Dol Common escape to safety over a garden wall. In this play Jonson is more concerned to expose the gulls than the rogues; and for five acts the rogues have so amused us with their ingenuity and high spirits that it would have been an artistic mistake to punish them too severely. *The Alchemist*, indeed, like *Bartholomew Fair*, is more comedy than satire.

The comparatively short-lived fashion for satirical plays about the turn of the century gains in interest when we remember that it apparently had some influence on Shakespeare. If we are to accept the case made out by Professor Oscar J. Campbell, we must be prepared to classify *Troilus and Cressida* as Shakespeare's 'comical satire'. This play has always been difficult to place in the canon. When it was first published in quarto it was described on the title-page as 'The Historie of Troylus and Cresseida', but in the preface to the reader it was several times referred to as a comedy. When Heminge and Condell were preparing the folio edition of the plays, *Troilus and Cressida* (owing probably to difficulties of copyright) was late in coming to their hands, and when they did obtain it they slipped it in without pagination at the head of the tragedies, and, ignoring the title-page of 1609, called it 'The Tragedie of Troylus and Cressida'. If we are willing to call it a comical satire, and if we further accept Professor Alexander's suggestion[1] that it was written for performance before a sophisticated inns-of-court audience, *Troilus and Cressida* becomes a good deal easier to understand. It has comparatively little action, but much debate and comment, often with a distinctly satirical turn. The Latinised and contorted language of many of the speeches approximates at times to that of Marston both in his plays and in his verse satires. The railing Thersites is of the same order as, say, Carlo Buffone in *Every Man out of his Humour*, or of Malevole in *The Malcontent*. Few readers are now disposed to regard the cynical treatment of the Trojan war and the satirical attitude to such warriors as Achilles, Nestor and Ajax as evidence that Shakespeare had lost faith in mankind, and was now passing through a period of gloom and disillusionment. If he had ever been blind to the intrigues of politicians or to the self-seeking motives which

often govern men's actions in public life he could not have
written the Histories. But how, it may be asked, are we
to interpret the love story of Troilus and the perjured
Cressida? Professor Campbell is in no doubt: Shakespeare
'meant their adventures to exemplify lust, and, therefore,
certain to lead them both to deserved disaster'.[1] Here, I
think, the scholar overplays his hand; it is not so simple as
that. There had always been an ironical streak in Shakespeare, a curious detachment that enabled him to shift his
point of view unexpectedly, and to look on at the ardours of
young lovers with eyes very different from their own, even
if a moment before he might seem to have imaginatively
identified himself with them. In *Romeo and Juliet* the
ironical attitude kept breaking in with Mercutio; it was to
reappear in Enobarbus contemplating two older lovers in
Egypt. In *Troilus and Cressida* this ironical detachment, like
much else in the play, is considerably exaggerated, passing
at times into the sardonic and the cynical. But ultimately
the difference is one of degree. In *Romeo and Juliet* Shakespeare gives us the lyrical passion of the lovers flecked
occasionally by the detached amusement of Mercutio and
the bawdy good nature of the Nurse. In *Troilus and Cressida*
the satirical note is dominant throughout, deepening into
the sardonic comments of that male nurse Pandarus and the
coarse scurrilities of Thersites, and yet suddenly changing
to the passionate speech of Troilus, and, I do not hesitate to
add, of Cressida. Professor Campbell, eagerly pursuing his
satirical quarry over fences and ditches, does not give
sufficient weight to those utterances of Troilus and of
Cressida. Since Shakespeare is so obviously being satirical
elsewhere in the play, he feels that Shakespeare must be

satirical here too. I cannot believe it. Whatever Shakespeare may have meant to do (and I am willing to believe that he was consciously writing a comical satire) he could not confine himself to that stylised and ultimately monotonous form all the time. Faced with two lovers, he rose, as always, to the occasion, and dignified them with the language of true passion, with the inevitable result that the scenes in which they appear belong to a quite different order of reality. We may say of those scenes that they jar upon the rest of the play, or we may say that the rest of the play jars upon those scenes. What we cannot say is that the language of Troilus is not the language of love. If we do, then I think Shakespeare himself might reply to us:

> If this be error, and upon me proved,
> I never writ, nor no man ever loved.

The speeches of Troilus—'O Pandarus, I tell thee, Pandarus', 'I am giddy, expectation whirls me round', and 'Injurious time, now with a robber's haste/Crams his rich thievery up'—might surely have come from the lips of Romeo, and Cressida's 'If I be false, or swerve a hair from truth' from those of Juliet.

As I interpret *Troilus and Cressida*, then, Shakespeare may well have set out to write a comical satire to amuse the worldly-wise and cynical young benchers of one of the inns-of-court, and may be said to have performed what he intended. But if Marston had been the author, the scenes between Troilus and Cressida would have been in keeping with the rest, and what in Shakespeare is a passionate love story would have been in Marston—what Professor Campbell apparently believes it to be in Shakespeare—no more than a lustful amour destined from its very nature to end miserably. The benchers might have liked it better Marston's way, but it was not the way of Shakespeare, whose infallible understanding of a human situation led him to

> Divert and crack, rend and deracinate

the unity of the satirical form with which he had experimented.

In that age of persistent raillery and invective, the Restoration period, we might expect the comic dramatists to provide us with a good deal of satire in their plays. So they do, but much of it is incidental, and little of it is of much account. Etherege shows some progress from the pure hedonism of his first play, *Love in a Tub*, to something approaching social criticism in his last play, *The Man of Mode*; but for Etherege, as for so many other comic dramatists of the period, the fashionable world was the only world, and the frivolous, intriguing, leisured life of Restoration society was ultimately the only good life. They might ridicule aberrations and eccentricities, or excesses and deficiencies in their own class, or laugh at aldermen and women of the Town; but they had no real quarrel, other than occasional boredom, with that world of which they were themselves among the leading ornaments, and which they mirrored with such amusement in their comedies.

The writer most relevant to our present concern is William Wycherley, and he is a difficult man to place. As a young man he led the same sort of life as the Dorimants and Bellmours and Mirabells of the contemporary comedy of manners; but it seems to have been generally felt by such capable judges as Dryden, Congreve, and John Dennis that he was a powerful satirist, one of the really big men of the period. A generation later, Steele could still find little to object to in *The Country Wife*,[1] but in the nineteenth century Macaulay singled Wycherley out for unqualified condemnation.[2] The twentieth century has, on the whole, accepted the estimate of Wycherley's contemporaries, and has seen him not as the most immoral of the Restoration dramatists, but as one who was uneasily aware of the moral vacuum in Restoration society, and who occasionally turned and rent that society with savage contempt.

Wycherley, I believe, was in a hopeless dilemma. He accepted—he had to accept—the fashionable world of his day, because it was the only world in which he could find sufficient intelligence and wit and culture to provide him with the intellectual and social milieu that a clever young man of his class required. He enjoyed, in his own way, the pleasures of this world, for which his wit and good looks and physical vigour so admirably suited him. But the intelligence, he discovered, did not go far enough, and was in any case not a complete answer to all the problems of life, and the gaiety was too often due to an empty head and an unfeeling heart, and fashionable society as a whole rested on a foundation of selfishness and hypocrisy. When he was *in* society he appears to have accepted its manners and morals without protest. We are told by one who knew him that 'pointed and severe as he was in his writings, in his temper he had all the softness of the tenderest disposition; gentle and inoffensive to every man in his particular character'.[3] It must therefore have been when he had withdrawn from the society of the fops and fine ladies and adventurers— when, in fact, he was alone with himself writing his plays— that the moral reaction came, and that he saw the fashionable world at its true value. It was then that he created his frightening succession of sensualists and hypocrites, Lady Flippant, Alderman Gripe, Vernish, Olivia, Horner, Lady Fidget, and the rest. In all Wycherley's work we have a sense of the divided mind: at one time he is the amused observer looking on with intelligent detachment, and at the next he is the angry moralist determined to expose the moral ulcers to our sight. The detachment of comedy is least present in *The Plain Dealer*, that play so extravagantly praised by Dryden as 'one of the most bold, most general, and most useful satires, which has ever been presented on the English theatre'.[1] I can willingly agree about the boldness; but the central situation is so loaded, and the character of Manly so peculiar, that the satire can hardly be described as either general or useful. If someone were to come forward with unquestionable evidence that the Manly-Olivia situation which Wycherley borrowed from Molière's *Le Misanthrope* was also autobiographical—that Wycherley, let us say, had gone off to fight at sea in one of the Dutch wars, and had returned to find his mistress living with his closest friend—I should not like *The Plain Dealer* any better, but I should feel that I could now account for its bitter and extravagant satire, and for the impression I have always had that the writer is crying out because he has been hurt.

With Congreve, on the other hand, we are in the presence of an artist who always seems to have his own feelings perfectly under control. He discriminates endlessly and fastidiously between fools and half-fools, and he exposes the weaknesses of the flesh no less than those of the mind. Congreve is willing enough to strike (and even allows himself occasionally a polished sneer at his audience); his plays are really addressed to the intelligent and contemptuous few, though he takes some pains with farcical action to make them enjoyable to the many. But his satire plays lightly and carelessly over manners—the bourgeois uxoriousness of Fondlewife, the empty chatter of a Tattle or a Witwoud, the vanity and affectation of Lady Wishfort, the inarticulate boorishness of Sir Wilful, and so on. Only once, in his second comedy, does he aim at anything more serious. Congreve, it has always seemed to me, having shown the Town in *The Old Bachelor* that he could be as gay and witty as Etherege, now set out in *The Double Dealer* to prove that he could be as serious and satirical as Wycherley. In Lady Touchwood and Maskwell he created two characters who could hardly be fitted into the framework of comedy, and who touch depths of wickedness that he never again attempted to sound.

Before leaving the Restoration I ought to mention one other famous play, Buckingham's *Rehearsal*, a dramatic skit which provides us with another good example of the value of an effective satirical form. So successful was the form of *The Rehearsal* (an author delightedly expounding the beauties of his play in rehearsal, while two unenchanted friends look on and make dry comments) that it was imitated several times, notably by Sheridan in *The Critic*. (In *Fanny's First Play* Shaw used the rehearsal situation again, but in a different way and with another purpose.) In *The Rehearsal* the dramatic author (in this case Dryden) is effectively ridiculed either by means of his naïve delight in his own absurdities, or by the simple device of making him avow openly the lowest possible motives for his various theatrical effects: his aesthetic standards are simply whatever goes.

Such satire, of course, will be all the more effective if there are reasonable grounds for supposing (as, indeed, there are with Dryden) that the charges made are not without some substance. But in our amusement at the sardonic comments of Smith and Johnson we probably do not pause to reflect that many of them are quite unfair, and that some of them could be equally well, or ill, applied to *Hamlet* or to *Paradise Lost*. Dryden, indeed, may have had the critical attitude of those two unimpressed spectators in mind when he argued in his 'Apology for Heroic Poetry and Poetic License' that it was unjust for those who had not the least notion of heroic writing to condemn the pleasure that other readers found in it merely because they themselves could not comprehend it. 'Are all the flights of Heroic Poetry', he asked, 'to be concluded bombast, unnatural, and mere madness, because *they* are not affected with their excellencies?'[1]

A fairer parody than either *The Rehearsal* or *The Critic* is William Whitehead's *Fatal Constancy: Or, Love in Tears*, a short but brilliant skit on the dreary platitudes of neo-classical tragedy. In this 'sketch of a tragedy in the heroic taste', interrupted 'with breaks and *et ceteras* (which are left to be supplied by the fancy of the reader)', Whitehead manages to ridicule in just over a hundred lines most of the conventions and clichés of this outworn drama. I quote the whole of Act III, where we have the stock description of Night, the 'Hark! she comes', the self-descriptive hero telling us about his feelings by enumerating their visible symptoms, the chronic substitution of talk for action, the elaborate and largely irrelevant simile in which blank verse gives way to rhymed couplets, and the hackneyed classical personifications of Cynthia, Pomona, and the rest.

ACT III

The Palmy Grove

The Hero, *Solus*

Night, black-brow'd Night, queen of the ebon wand,
Now o'er the world has spread her solemn reign.
The glow-worm twinkles, and from every flower
The pearly dews return the pale reflex
Of Cynthia's beams, each drop a little moon!
Hark! Lindamira comes—No, 'twas the breath
Of Zephyr panting on the leafy spray.
Perhaps he lurks in yonder woodbine bower
To steal soft kisses from her lips, and catch
Ambrosial odours from her passing sighs.
O thief!—
    She comes; quick let us haste away.
The guards pursue us? Heavens!—Come then, my love,
Fly, fly this moment.
       [*Here a long conference upon love, virtue, the Moon,
       etc. till the guards come up.*]
    —Dogs, will ye tear her from me?
You must not, shall not—O, my heart-strings crack,
My head turns round, my starting eye-balls hang
Upon her parting steps—I can no more.—
    So the first man, from Paradise exil'd,
With fond reluctance leaves the blooming wild:
Around the birds in pleasing concert sing,
Beneath his feet th' unbidden flow'rets spring;
On verdant hills the flocks unnumber'd play,
Through verdant hills meand'ring rivers stray;
Blossoms and fruits at once the trees adorn,
Eternal roses bloom on every thorn,
And join Pomona's lap to Amalthaea's horn.
       [*Exeunt, torn off on different sides.*][1]

It is distressing to reflect how little Whitehead has had to
travesty the actual to produce this absurdity.

In the hands of such writers as Horace and James Smith or Sir Max Beerbohm parody can be a delightful form of criticism. There ought, however, to be some weakness to expose: some inadequacy of thought or feeling, or some fixed mannerism of expression. Keats, who was a fine judge of his own work, was unwilling to publish *Isabella* because he felt it was too vulnerable to criticism. 'It is possible to write fine things which cannot be laugh'd at in any way', he wrote to a friend. 'Isabella is what I should call were I a reviewer "A weak-sided Poem" with an amusing sober-sadness about it.'[1] It was, in fact, a poem that rather invited parody. The parodies in the *Rejected Addresses* of Horace and James Smith are not all equally effective, for various reasons, but the poem they wrote for Crabbe is brilliant.

> John Richard William Alexander Dwyer
> Was footman to Justinian Stubbs, Esquire...

catches perfectly Crabbe's forthright manner of stating his facts, the occasional flatness of his couplets, his tendency to rhyme on an unimportant syllable, and his fearlessly prosaic choice of names for his characters. Again, the episode of the playbill fluttering down through the theatre until it settles on a musician's wig comes very close to Crabbe's odd mixture of honest homespun and the more poetic diction of the eighteenth century.

> Perchance, while pit and gallery cry, 'Hats off,'
> And awed Consumption checks his chided cough,
> Some giggling daughter of the Queen of Love
> Drops, reft of pin, her play-bill from above;
> Like Icarus, while laughing galleries clap,
> Soars, ducks, and dives in air the printed scrap;
> But, wiser far than he, combustion fears,

And, as it flies, eludes the chandeliers;
Till sinking gradual, with repeated twirl,
It settles, curling, on a fiddler's curl;
Who, from his powder'd pate the intruder strikes,
And, for mere malice, sticks it on the spikes.

There again we have Crabbe's undivided concentration on
the fact, and in such lines as 'Soars, ducks, and dives in air
the printed scrap' or in such an expression as 'his chided
cough', his firm and precise use of language. The whole
passage is far from being a travesty; it might have been
written by some earnest and promising novice of the school
of Crabbe.

Parody, on the other hand, can quite easily be nothing
more than a vulgar and degrading travesty of the original,
which has as little relation to satire as Thomas Rymer's
sarcastic observations on *Othello* have to criticism. In spite
of what Keats says, fine things *can* be laughed at, and frequently are. Satirical criticism is only too easy; and in recent
years it has been frequently employed by critics who have
wished to run down one kind of poetry (usually Romantic)
so that they might set up another kind that they like better.
The strange idea that poetry ought to be 'tough', that the
poem should carry within itself some ironical prophylactic to
the laughter of irreverent readers, is one that had never, I
imagine, occurred to anyone until the present century. In
an essay written some years ago, Mr Robert Penn Warren
comes very near to suggesting that poetry is what cannot be
parodied, and he exerts himself to show how wrong we all
were in enjoying one of the best-known of Shelley's lyrics,
'An Indian Serenade'. Mr Warren's handling of this poem
is in the best Rymer tradition, though he adds a refinement

by managing to misquote Shelley on one occasion in order to make his point.* The truth is that any poem can be burlesqued or parodied or made fun of, and there are always plenty of insensitive people who will be amused.

Eighteenth-century comedy does not contain much that can be called satire, although of course there were satirical strokes in Sheridan, and Goldsmith in both of his comedies offered some shrewd ridicule of the fashionable sentimental drama. More to the point, however, is *The Beggar's Opera* of John Gay, where Sir Robert Walpole was effectively satirised. In his burlesques and farces Fielding addressed himself to the various follies and fashions of the day, and in *The Historical Register* and *Pasquin* attacked political corruption so dangerously that he drove Walpole to bring in the Licensing Act. (It is worth remarking that in both of these plays Fielding used again the form of *The Rehearsal*.)

I now leap over a dramatic vacuum, and come finally to Bernard Shaw. Shaw answers perfectly to my description of the satirist. From his first play to his last he was never content to accept or to tolerate what he found; he was concerned to expose what he believed to be evil or moribund or absurd or illogical in the modern world, and more particularly, of course, in England. He was bent on changing men's minds, and nearly always he was willing to subordinate

---

* Reprinted in R. W. Stallman, *Critiques and Essays in Criticism, 1920–1948* (1949), pp. 85 ff. 'We remember', Mr Warren tells us, '...how the Champak's odors "pine"'. Mr Warren's memory has betrayed him: the Champak odours *fail*. (Mr Stallman repeats the error.) Mr Warren's willingness to be fair to Shelley may be gauged from the following (my italic): 'How does the lover get to the chamber window? He *refuses to say* how, in his semi-somnambulistic daze, he got there. He *blames*, he says, a "spirit in my feet", and *hastens to disavow* any knowledge of how that spirit operates.' This is surely the very voice of Thomas Rymer.

a remarkable gift for comedy to the moral and social and philosophical ideas he wished to express. This is not to say that he did not get a lot of enjoyment out of exposing muddle and confusion and stupidity. There is a pleasure in being clear-headed that only the clear-headed know. He enjoyed, too, pursuing an idea to its logical conclusion, and he obviously took considerable pleasure in playing with ideas, even clowning with them, and acting the intellectual buffoon. Happily for all of us, the artist in him was never brow-beaten by the moralist, and his high spirits and affability were a perpetual wonder and delight. In the preface to *Plays Unpleasant* he runs rapidly over all the things he most detested: popular morality, popular religion, 'violence and slaughter, whether in war, sport, or the butcher's yard', the fashionable moneyed class, and a good deal else. 'I was neither a sceptic nor a cynic in these matters,' he explains; 'I simply understood life differently from the average respectable man; and as I certainly enjoyed myself more—mostly in ways which would have made him unbearably miserable—I was not splenetic over our variance.' It was this absence of spleen, this unfailing good-nature, that humanised Shaw's reforming zeal, and gained for his satire the unwilling attention of several generations of playgoers. In the words of another Irishman,

> Truth from his lips prevail'd with double sway,
> And fools that came to scoff remained to pray.

Goldsmith's parson, with his 'meek and unaffected grace', will not do for Shaw, of course, but the parson's technique of salvation is Shavian enough:

> He tried each art, reprov'd each dull delay,
> Allur'd to brighter worlds, and led the way.

'He tried each art.' Shaw was very far from confining himself to ridicule. He argued and exhorted in both plays and prefaces, he touched the conscience by simple exposure of evils, he showed in the Caesar of his *Caesar and Cleopatra*, what a fully civilized man might be, he worked by paradox and epigram and by the relentless pursuit of a human situation to its necessary conclusion. But invariably he kept the audience in the forefront of his consciousness, and all the time he wrought on 'those guilty creatures sitting at a play'. His art was essentially an art of persuasion. What Shaw wrote of Ibsen is true of himself. He was the master of 'a terrible art of sharp-shooting at the audience, trapping them, fencing with them, aiming always at the sorest spot in their consciences.... When you despise something you ought to take off your hat to, or admire and imitate something you ought to loathe, you cannot resist the dramatist who knows how to touch those morbid spots in you, and make you see that they are morbid.' If Shaw is not much read by the younger generation, it may be that his reputation is at present in that stretch of slack water which is usually reached shortly after a writer's death, and from which he may be expected to emerge in due course. But if he is comparatively neglected today, it may equally well be because he did his work so well, and the causes for which he battled have almost all been won. Neglect in such a case is the measure of success.

VII

CONCLUSION

IT must now be evident that English satire is remarkably varied, and that it springs from many different motives. The earlier satirists were rather fond of taking a high line and referring to satire as a 'sacred weapon'; and there is no reason to doubt that much satire is the outcome of honest indignation at vice or folly, and of a desire to promote the public good. But we need not assume that the satirist's motives are invariably noble, or that his satire is always public spirited. Without ourselves becoming satirical, we can probably agree that the one constant element in satire is the relief, or even pleasure, that it gives to the satirist. When, for example, Henry Fox, Lord Holland, built for himself in his old age an imitation classical villa, and ornamented the grounds with sham ruins, Thomas Gray's contempt for the man and all his works overflowed in some of the most devastating lines ever written by an English satirist:

> Old and abandoned by each venal friend
>   Here H[olland] took the pious resolution
> To smuggle some few years and strive to mend
>   A broken character and constitution.
>
> On this congenial spot he fix'd his choice,
>   Earl Godwin trembled for his neighbouring sand,
> Here Seagulls scream and cormorants rejoice,
>   And Mariners tho' shipwreckt dread to land;
>
> Here reigns the blustring north and blighting east,
>   No tree is heard to whisper, bird to sing,

Yet nature cannot furnish out the feast,
  Art he invokes new horrors still to bring.

Now mouldring fanes and battlements arise,
  Arches and turrets nodding to their fall,
Unpeopled palaces delude his eyes,
  And mimick desolation covers all.

Ah, said the sighing Peer, had Bute been true,
  Nor Shelburn's, Rigby's, Calcroft's friendship vain,
Far other scenes than these had bless'd our view
  And realised the ruins that we feign.

Purg'd by the sword and beautifyed by fire,
  Then had we seen proud London's hated walls,
Owls might have hooted in St Peter's Quire,
  And foxes stunk and litter'd in St. Paul's.[1]

Gray's disgust with the tasteless absurdity of Lord Holland's artificial ruins coalesces with a deeper loathing of his unprincipled political career and his grasping, money-loving character. This scathing attack was fully justified, but Gray's lines were written primarily as a means of relief for his own outraged feelings. If they have a further value, that comes from our delight in watching the masterly play of the satirical weapon; but if Lord Holland had been a man of taste and a public benefactor we should still experience that delight.

Satire, in fact, is not always and necessarily enlisted in the cause of truth and virtue. It was a favourite idea of the eighteenth century that ridicule is the test of truth. 'Nothing is ridiculous,' Shaftesbury had argued, 'except what is deformed; nor is anything proof against raillery except what is handsome and just.'[2] Whatever validity those words may have in the realm of philosophy, they have little relevance to the world of action: a Socrates can be ridiculed as easily as a Lord Holland. Dryden, Pope, and Swift were all capable at times of using their satirical skill to ridicule someone who was not culpable at all, or to pour contempt on something they happened to dislike. All three were masters of denigration; and though they are usually to be found fighting on the side of truth, they can be just as devastating when they happen to be attacking it. The satirist has a responsibility to truth and justice which he rarely manages to fulfil all the time, and if he becomes involved in party strife we must expect his vision of the truth to become blurred or distorted.

Still, the majority of satirists normally attack what they at least believe to be bad or untrue. Even so, it may be asked, how effective is satire as a means of reforming morals and manners? 'The preaching of divines', Swift once remarked, 'helps to preserve well-inclined men in the course of virtue, but seldom or never reclaims the vicious.'[1] If preaching does as much as that, it does a good deal, and a similar claim may be made for satire. Certain kinds of satirical writing (political satire is a good example) are not normally intended to convert one's opponents, but to gratify and fortify one's friends. Satire has performed a useful function if it only cheers on the faithful.

It also may, and it sometimes does, bring over those who are not definitely committed or not actively hostile. It is true that we all tend to set up an immediate resistance to the satirist when we realise that his satire may apply to ourselves; but if we think that satire must for that reason be ineffective we probably underestimate the extent to which even unwelcome ideas can penetrate our defences. We may believe that we have suppressed them, only to find that they are still there beneath the surface. Satire, in fact, is often active below the level of consciousness, and may therefore work by delayed action.

But can the satirist ever hope to reclaim the vicious? The poet Cowper, for one, was sceptical about the possibility of reformation by such means. He was ready to believe that the Addisonian variety of satire, which aimed at the correction of manners rather than morals, had the best chance of success.

> Yet what can satire, whether grave or gay?
> It may correct a foible, may chastise
> The freaks of fashion, regulate the dress,
> Retrench a swordblade, or displace a patch;
> But where are its sublimer trophies found?
> What vice has it subdued? what heart reclaimed
> By rigour? or whom laughed into reform?
> Alas! Leviathan is not so tamed....[1]

Satire works effectively in the rather limited field that Cowper prescribes for it because men and women—and more especially those who move in the world of fashion, or in intellectual and artistic coteries—are particularly sensitive to ridicule, especially when it is directed to showing that their affectations and fashions are really rather unintelligent, or, worse still, *démodé*.

But must we abandon all claims for satire as a deterrent to the more serious moral offences? If the satirist cannot often reclaim the vicious, there is a good case to be made for his discouraging them, for his creating an astringent atmosphere in which it is less easy for them to flourish. Yet why, it may be asked, can the wicked not be dealt with by the normal process of the law? For an answer to that question we may go again to Swift. 'It is very plain', he once wrote,

that considering the defectiveness of our laws, the weakness of the prerogative, or the cunning of ill-designing men, it is possible that many great abuses may be visibly committed which cannot be legally punished.... I am apt to think it was to supply such defects as these that satire was first introduced into the world, whereby those whom neither religion nor natural virtue nor fear of punishment were able to keep within the bounds of their duty, might be withheld by the shame of having their crimes exposed to open view in the strongest colours, and themselves rendered odious to mankind.[1]

For Pope, too, as for Swift, it seemed almost a sacred duty to

> Brand the bold Front of shameless, guilty Men,
> Dash the proud Gamester in his gilded Car,
> Bare the mean Heart that lurks beneath a Star...
> Yes, while I live, no rich or noble knave
> Shall walk the World, in credit, to his grave.[2]

Pope, like Swift, is thinking more especially of those whom the law has failed to restrain, either because there is no law in the statute book that can be applied to their offence, or because by rank or wealth or privilege they are above the reach of the law. Such men, Pope believed, could still be checked by satire—

> Safe from the Bar, the Pulpit, and the Throne,
> Yet touch'd and sham'd by *Ridicule* alone.[3]

We may have reduced the number of those individuals in the twentieth century, but we are still far from having eliminated them.

In making those confident claims for the corrective effect of his satirical poetry Pope is obviously thinking of personal rather than general satire. He wrote both kinds, but his own

preference was for the personal. To Arbuthnot, who wrote
to him on his deathbed asking him to continue in his 'noble
disdain and abhorrence of vice', but to 'study more to
reform than to chastise',[1] Pope replied that the one was
hardly feasible without the other. It would, he explained,
be more agreeable to his nature to avoid the personal attack:

But General Satire in Times of General Vice has no force, and
is no punishment: People have ceased to be ashamed of it when
so many are joind with them; and 'tis only by hunting one or two
from the Herd that any Examples can be made. If a man writ
all his Life against the Collective Body of the Banditti, or against
Lawyers, would it do the least Good, or lessen the Body? But if
some are hung up, or pilloryed, it may prevent others. And in
my low Station, with no other Power than this, I hope to deter,
if not to reform.[2]

In re-writing this letter for publication, Pope considerably
amplified his argument in favour of personal satire:

To reform and not to chastise, I am afraid is impossible, and
that the best Precepts, as well as the best Laws, would prove of
small use, if there were no Examples to inforce them. To attack
Vices in the abstract, without touching Persons, may be safe
fighting indeed, but it is fighting with Shadows. General
propositions are obscure, misty, and uncertain, compar'd with
plain, full, and home examples.... The only sign by which I
found my writings ever did any good, or had any weight, has
been that they raised the anger of bad men. And my greatest
comfort, and encouragement to proceed, has been to see that
those who have no shame, and no fear, of any thing else, have
appear'd touch'd by my Satires.[3]

We are not here concerned with whether personal satire was,
or was not, painful to Pope; it is unlikely that it hurt him
more than it hurt his victims. But his general defence of
personal satire is sound enough. Pope seeks to justify it not

because it reforms the vicious, but because exposing the evil-doer has a deterrent effect on others, as the farmer hangs up the crow he has shot, or as the heads of traitors were formerly displayed to public view on Temple Bar.

But satire functions effectively on many different levels; we need not rest the case for it only on such desperate or such personal examples. If general satire is less immediate in its effect than the direct exposure of an individual, it may still serve to keep us from compromising with bad practices, or from growing so accustomed to evil and folly that we come in time to be unconscious of them, or to accept them as natural and inevitable. By enlisting the moral disapproval of society against the offence, no less than the offender, the satirist can help to maintain the standards of a civilised community. By refusing to compromise with wrong-doing and wrong-thinking, with shoddy behaviour and shoddy art, by his very insistence on drawing attention to them whenever they occur, he keeps ethical and social and aesthetic values from being insensibly lowered or lost by default. He knows, too, that our standards are threatened quite as much by the slow spread of mediocrity as by the flagrant offence which every-one can see and repudiate, and he will therefore be vigilant in his exposure of the charlatan, the *ersatz*, and the second-rate. Above all, the satirist today will not be likely to forget how easily and imperceptibly things may go wrong. Living in the twentieth century, he will readily understand why Pope recalled to the readers of the *Dunciad*,

what the Dutch stories somewhere relate, that a great part of their Provinces was once overflow'd by a small opening made in one of their dykes by a single *water-rat*.[1]

NOTES

PAGE 1

1 *The Observer*, 22 July 1956.

PAGE 2

1 *Laughter. An Essay on the Meaning of the Comic* (1913), pp. 8 ff.

PAGE 4

1 *The Quintessence of Ibsenism* (1929 ed.), p. 186.

PAGE 7

1 *Opere* (1729), p. 120.
2 *The Governour* (Everyman ed.), p. 58.

PAGE 8

1 *Elizabethan Critical Essays*, ed. G. Gregory Smith (1904), I, pp. 176 f.

PAGE 9

1 *Op. cit.* Introduction.
2 *Amendments of Mr. Collier's False and Imperfect Citations, etc.* (1698), p. 8.
3 *A Short Vindication of the Relapse* (1698); *Dramatic Essays of the Neoclassic Age*, ed. H. H. Adams and B. Hathaway (1950), p. 192.

PAGE 10

1 *The Complete Works of George Savile, Marquess of Halifax*, ed. Walter Raleigh (1912), p. 193.

PAGE 11

1 *Ibid.* pp. 203 f.
2 *Love of Fame, the Universal Passion*, Preface; *Poetical Works* (1852), I, p. 55.

PAGE 12

1 *Biographia Literaria*, ed. J. Shawcross (1907), II, p. 6.
2 *Ibid.* p. 123.

PAGE 13

1 *The Collected Poems of W. H. Davies* (1928), p. 80.

PAGE 16

1 *Essays of John Dryden*, ed W. P. Ker (1900), I, p. 155.

PAGE 17

1 *Some Materials towards Memoirs of the Reign of King George II*, *by John, Lord Hervey*, ed. Romney Sedgwick (1931), II, pp. 488 f.

PAGE 19

1 Samuel Johnson, *Lives of the English Poets*, ed. G. Birkbeck Hill (1905), II, p. 380.

2 *Appreciations* (1889), pp. 65 ff.

PAGE 20

1 *Elizabethan Critical Essays*, ed. cit. I, pp. 184 f.

2 David Worcester, *The Art of Satire* (1940), p. 16.

PAGE 23

1 See G. R. Owst, *Literature and Pulpit in Medieval England* (1933).

PAGE 24

1 Jonathan Swift, 'On the Poor Man's Contentment', *Works* (1766), XIII, p. 24.

2 'Thoughts upon Various Subjects', *Miscellanies. The Second Volume* (1727), p. 345.

PAGE 25

1 *Twelve Sermons Preached upon Several Occasions . . . The Second Edition* (1697), I, p. 458.

PAGE 26

1 *The Poems of William Dunbar*, ed. W. MacKay Mackenzie (1932), p. 9.
Translation:
Lean, impotent fellow, sluggard, lousy both in flank and back;
Fie! withered skin, you are but wart and wrinkle . . .
Henpecked coward, no man values you at a [piece of] cress,
Lazy, idle(?) great lout, swine-herd ever for small beer.

2 *Letters*, ed. M. B. Forman (1935), p. 51.

PAGE 27

1 *Op. cit.* (1743 ed.), III, ll. 85 f.

PAGE 28

1 *The Complete Poems of John Skelton*, ed. Philip Henderson (1931), p. 326.

PAGE 29

1 *Ibid.*

PAGE 31

1 See John Peter, 'This word satyre', *Review of English Studies* (1955), new series, VI, pp. 288 ff.

2 *Elizabethan Critical Essays*, ed. cit. II, p. 27.

3 *Ibid.* p. 209.

PAGE 32

1 'A Postscript to the Reader', *The Collected Poems of Joseph Hall*, ed. A. Davenport (1949), p. 97.

2 *Ibid.* p. 33.

PAGE 35

1 *The Marprelate Tracts, 1588, 1589*, ed. William Pierce (1911), p. 154.

2 *English Literature in the Sixteenth Century, excluding Drama* (1954), p. 412.

PAGE 36

1 *The Intelligencer*, no. iii

2 Act II.

PAGE 37

1 *Minor Poets of the Caroline Period*, ed. George Saintsbury (1921), III, pp. 57 f.

PAGE 39

1 *The Poems and Letters of Andrew Marvell*, ed. H. M. Margoliouth (1952), I, p. 201.

PAGE 41

1 Robert Wolseley, Preface to *Valentinian*, *Critical Essays of the Seventeenth Century*, ed. J. E. Spingarn (1909), III, p. 13.

2 *Op. cit.* (ed. 1743), II, ll. 99 f.

NOTES

PAGE 44

1 *On Modern Literature*, ed. Terence Spencer and James Sutherland (1955), p. 7.

PAGE 45

1 *The Duellist*, III, ll. 129 ff.; *Poetical Works*, ed. Douglas Grant (1956), p. 280.
2 'To — After reading a Life and Letters.'
3 'Lines to Edward Fitzgerald.'

PAGE 46

1 I am indebted to Mr T. R. Henn for drawing my attention to this poem.

PAGE 48

1 X, ll. 217 f.
2 III, l. 321.
3 *Lives of the Poets*, ed. G. Birkbeck Hill, I, p. 447.
4 *Essays*, ed. Ker, II, pp. 67 ff.
5 *Ibid.* p. 92.

PAGE 49

1 *Op. cit.* ll. 18 ff.

PAGE 50

1 *Op. cit.* l. 70.
2 *Essays*, ed. Ker, II, p. 80.

PAGE 51

1 Joseph Spence, *Anecdotes*, ed. S. W. Singer (1820), pp. 171 f.

PAGE 52

1 *Op. cit.* ll. 620 f.

PAGE 53

1 *Essays*, ed. Ker, II, p. 93.
1 *Op. cit.* ll. 152 f., 173 f.
1 *Advancement of Learning*, book II.

PAGE 54

1 *Op. cit.* ll. 8 ff.

PAGE 55
1 Ian Jack, *Augustan Satire* (1952), p. 52.
2 *Essays*, ed. Ker, II, p. 80.
3 See R. Jack Smith, 'Shadwell's impact upon John Dryden,' *Review of English Studies*, 1944, XX, pp. 29 ff.
4 'Preface prefix'd to the five imperfect Editions of the *Dunciad*'; *Poems* (Twickenham ed.), V, p. 205.

PAGE 56
1 *Op. cit.* ll. 15 ff.

PAGE 57
1 *Ibid.* ll. 25 ff.

PAGE 58
1 *An Essay on the Genius and Writings of Pope* (1782 ed.), I, p. 254.
2 *Ibid.* p. 344.

PAGE 59
1 *Op. cit.* II, ll. 103 ff.
2 *Ibid.* I, l. 138.

PAGE 60
1 *Op. cit.* II, ll. 123 ff.
2 *Biographia Literaria*, ed. J. Shawcross, II, p. 5 (ch. xiv).
3 W. K. Wimsatt, 'The Augustan mode in English poetry', *ELH* (1953), XX, p. 9.

PAGE 61
1 *Op. cit.* I, ll. 225 ff.

PAGE 62
1 *Op. cit.* III, ll. 199 f.

PAGE 63
1 *Ibid.* ll. 209 f.

PAGE 64
1 *Essay on Criticism*, ll. 653 f.

PAGE 65
1 *Moral Essays*, II ('Epistle to a Lady'), ll. 235 ff.

PAGE 66

1 *The Pursuits of Literature*, IV, l. 89n.

PAGE 68

1 *An Epistle to the Right Honourable William Pulteney, Esq.*
ll. 167ff.

PAGE 70

1 *The Task*, VI ('The Winter Walk at Noon'), ll. 270ff.

PAGE 71

1 *Ibid.* II ('The Garden'), ll. 150ff.

PAGE 72

1 *Miscellanies in Prose and Verse* (1713), p. 234.

PAGE 73

1 *The Task*, II ('The Time-Piece'), ll. 639ff.

PAGE 75

1 *His very Self and Voice: Collected Conversations of Lord Byron*,
ed. Ernest J. Lovell (1954), p. 350.

PAGE 79

1 R. W. Chambers, *Thomas More* (1935), p. 131.

PAGE 80

1 See *The Batchelars Banquet*, ed. F. P. Wilson (1929), pp. ixff.

PAGE 82

1 *Bibliotheca Curiosa. Some Political Satires of the Seventeenth
Century*, ed. E. Goldsmid (1885), I, pp. 59f.

PAGE 86

1 This is less true of his verse than of his prose. In his verse
Swift frequently satirises the individual.

PAGE 87

1 *Journal to Stella*, ed. Harold Williams (1948), I, p. 162.

PAGE 89

1 'Epistle to a Lady', ll. 203ff.; *The Poems of Jonathan Swift*,
ed. Harold Williams (1937), II, p. 636.

PAGE 91

1 *Vanessa and her Correspondence with Jonathan Swift*, ed. A. Martin Freeman (1921), p. 129.

2 *Miscellanies. The Second Volume* (1727), p. 344.

PAGE 92

1 Joseph Spence, *Anecdotes, Observations, and Characters of Books and Men*, ed. S. W. Singer (1820), pp. 19f.

PAGE 97

1 If I were asked why Swift sent him to Emmanuel, I might answer, Why not? If that reply were thought insufficient, I could add what I did not know till Mr H. S. Bennett told me, that Swift's patron Sir William Temple was for some years a fellow-commoner at Emmanuel.

PAGE 100

1 *The Present State of Wit*, ed. Donald F. Bond (1947) (Augustan Reprint Society), p. 3.

PAGE 102

1 *Op. cit.* ch. XLVI (Everyman ed.), p. 323.

PAGE 103

1 Henry Festing Jones, *Samuel Butler, Author of Erewhon. A Memoir* (1920), I, p. 152.

PAGE 104

1 *Op. cit.* ch. xxii.

PAGE 110

1 Bk. I, ch. xii.

PAGE 113

1 Bk. IV, ch. viii.

PAGE 115

1 *On Modern Literature*, ed. Terence Spencer and James Sutherland (1955), p. 242.

PAGE 117

1 Ch. xviii.

NOTES

PAGE 118
1 *Ibid.*
2 Ch. ii.

PAGE 119
1 *The Works of Jane Austen*, ed. R. W. Chapman (1954), VI, p. 86.
2 *Ibid.* pp. 77f.

PAGE 121
1 *Letters*, ed. M. B. Forman (1948), p. 228.

PAGE 122
1 Emile Legouis and Louis Cazamian, *A History of English Literature* (1934), p. 1120.

PAGE 123
1 *Thomas Love Peacock* (1927), p. 196.

PAGE 126
1 *Vanity Fair*, ch. xvii.

PAGE 127
1 *Op. cit.* ch. xxxix.

PAGE 128
1 *Ibid.* ch. xl.

PAGE 129
1 *Ibid.* ch. xxiv.
2 Vol. I, ch. xii.

PAGE 134
1 E. K. Chambers, *The Elizabethan Stage* (1923), I, p. 243.

PAGE 135
1 *Ibid.* pp. 127f.

PAGE 136
1 *Essays of John Dryden*, ed. Ker, II, p. 67.
2 Chambers, *op. cit.* I, p. 295.

PAGE 137
1 Act V, sc. i.

PAGE 138
1 *Elizabethan Critical Essays*, ed. G. Gregory Smith, I, p. 176.

PAGE 139

1 *Shakespeare's Life and Art* (1938), p. 195.

PAGE 140

1 Oscar J. Campbell, *Shakespeare's Satire* (1943), p. 110.

PAGE 143

1 See *Tatler*, no. iii, 16 April 1709. Steele, however, objected to Etherege's *The Man of Mode* in *Spectator*, no. lxv, 15 May 1711.
2 *Critical and Historical Essays* (1866), III, pp. 235 ff.
3 George Granville, Lord Lansdowne, *The Genuine Works in Verse and Prose* (1732), I, p. 434.

PAGE 144

1 *Essays*, ed. Ker, I, p. 182.

PAGE 146

1 *Essays*, ed. Ker, I, p. 182.

PAGE 147

1 *The Works of the English Poets*, ed. Alexander Chalmers (1810), XVII, p. 251.

PAGE 148

1 *Letters*, ed. cit. p. 391.

PAGE 154

1 The text is that given in *Correspondence of Thomas Gray*, ed. Paget Toynbee and Leonard Whibley (1935), III, p. 1262.
2 'Freedom of Wit and Humour', *Characteristics*, ed. J. M. Robertson (1900), I, p. 85.

PAGE 155

1 *Miscellanies in Prose and Verse. The First Volume* (1727), p. 404.

PAGE 156

1 *The Task* ('The Time-Piece'), ll. 315 ff.

PAGE 157

1 *The Examiner*, no. xxxviii.
2 *The First Satire of the Second Book of Horace Imitated*, ll. 106 ff., 119 f.
3 *Epilogue to the Satires*, II, ll. 210 f.

NOTES

PAGE 158

1 *The Correspondence of Alexander Pope*, ed. George Sherburn (1956), III, p. 417.
2 *Ibid.* p. 423.
3 *Ibid.* p. 419.

PAGE 159

1 *The Dunciad, in Three Books with Notes Variorum* (1729), III, l. 337n.

INDEX

INDEX

INDEX

INDEX